Graduate CVs and C

Palgrave Career Skills

Graduate CVs and Covering Letters

Bruce Woodcock and Jenny Keaveney

 macmillan education palgrave

First published 2017 by
PALGRAVE

Palgrave in the UK is an imprint of Macmillan Publishers Limited, registered in England, company number 785998, of 4 Crinan Street, London, N1 9XW.

Palgrave® and Macmillan® are registered trademarks in the United States, the United Kingdom, Europe and other countries.

ISBN 978–1–137–60626–6 paperback

This book is printed on paper suitable for recycling and made from fully managed and sustained forest sources. Logging, pulping and manufacturing processes are expected to conform to the environmental regulations of the country of origin.

A catalogue record for this book is available from the British Library.

A catalog record for this book is available from the Library of Congress.

Dedication

Bruce
To my wonderful wife and sons: Beth, Gavin and Ewan

Jenny
To Arthur

Contents

CHAPTER 13
Mind the gap – and other CV problems   151

CHAPTER 14
Job hunting tips and how to submit your CV   165

Introduction

Why will this book be useful to you?

As university careers advisers we receive vast numbers of queries about CVs, from students and graduates applying for anything from part-time casual jobs to postdoctoral research posts.

Although there are many books on CV writing, it can be hard for students and recent graduates to find one that relates specifically to them. Most books on CVs are written either for non-graduates or for experienced managers and staff.

This book aims to fill that gap by offering advice targeted towards students and recent graduates. Whether you are applying for a part-time or summer job, an internship or placement, or a graduate training scheme, this book will help you to write an effective CV that will make you stand out to employers.

It is not easy for students and graduates to find the right job. The Association of Graduate Recruiters' annual survey carried out in 2015 (http://www.agr.org.uk/surveys) showed an average of 65 applications for every graduate scheme vacancy. In popular areas such as the media or investment banking, employers will receive over a hundred CVs for every job! The increasing demand for graduates to demonstrate employability skills and work experience in addition to their academic achievement, and the need for many students to earn money to support themselves through their studies, means that this high level of competition has trickled down to even casual and part-time jobs.

A quality CV will not only help you to stand out from other candidates but can also help you to learn more about your skills and other attributes.

What is a CV?

CV stands for '*curriculum vitae*', a Latin phrase which translates literally as 'course of life'. A more useful and detailed definition is:

> 💬 A summary of a job applicant's experience and educational background, together with other relevant information about the candidate. 💬

You may also see the word 'résumé' used as an alternative for 'CV'. It is derived from the French word which means 'condensed account' or 'summary'. This is the standard term in the USA, where they generally drop the accents and just write 'resume' but still keep the French pronunciation ('re-zoom-ay' rather than 'rez-yoom'). Slightly strangely, the usual term in France is 'CV', not 'résumé'.

The word 'summary' gives a better idea of what a CV actually is than does 'course of life'. A CV is not the same thing as a life story or autobiography. The information it provides is selected and focused, with the purpose of demonstrating to the employer that you are a good candidate for the job.

Perhaps the first CV ever written was the one used by Leonardo da Vinci over 500 years ago to apply for a position at the court of Ludovico Sforza, the Duke of Milan. You can find it online at http://www.mycareertopia.com/resume-secrets-davinci-cv. Considering how long ago it was written, it is very good: it is concise and Leonardo designed it to market himself to the duke by highlighting the skills he could offer in military engineering. Not surprisingly, he got the job!

Leonardo's CV was more of a letter of application than what we would call a CV today. The modern CV sets out the candidate's experience, qualifications, and so on, much more briefly, using headings, bullet points and a note format to allow the reader to take in as much information as possible at a glance.

Your CV is more than just a 'summary of your education and experience'. It is a marketing document; an advert that sells you to an employer by showcasing your unique set of skills and attributes. To be successful, you need to make it as relevant as possible to the job and the employer.

When should you use a CV?

A CV will not be acceptable for every job application. Many employers, particularly large employers running graduate recruitment schemes and also most public sector employers, will use their own application form. In these cases, you will not normally be expected to send a CV as well. And, if you are asked to fill out one of these application forms, don't ever try to send a CV instead! The employer will have spent a lot of time designing the form in a way that allows them to get the information they need about candidates and to compare candidates quickly and easily – so if an applicant can't be bothered to fill out the form, the employer will not be bothered to read his or her CV!

CVs, though, are commonly used by smaller employers, employers in the media and creative sectors, and recruitment agencies. It is therefore always useful to have a CV ready to use when, for example, you are applying for part-time and vacation jobs during your studies or if you are applying for a graduate job or internship with an employer that does ask for a CV. You can also use a CV to make speculative approaches – contacting employers who have not advertised a vacancy but who you hope may be able to offer you a suitable job or work experience.

Preparing a CV and keeping it up to date does not only mean that you always have a document ready to send out quickly when needed. Summarising and writing down your skills and achievements will also help you to get an insight into what might suit you and to plan your career development.

How do student and graduate CVs differ from other CVs?

Parents sometimes give well-meaning advice to their offspring on how they should write a CV. Unless you are lucky enough to have a parent who works in graduate recruitment, this advice may not always be helpful. Not only can it be out of date, if it has been a long time since your mum or dad applied for a job, but also their advice could be appropriate for someone already in work, but not for a student. Although CVs for students and graduates do have a number of factors in common with other CVs, there are some differences of emphasis.

Student and graduate CVs often put the greatest emphasis on their degree. Depending on whether your course of study is relevant to the job you are applying for, you may include quite detailed information on modules studied, dissertations, individual and group projects and technical skills gained.

This information about your education will normally come before any work experience, because work is often a less important element than on the CV of an experienced employee.

If you don't have any work experience that is directly relevant to the jobs you are applying for, you can compensate by including skills you have gained outside your course. This could be through vacation and part-time jobs, posts of responsibility in student societies, sports teams or university positions such as student ambassador or course representative.

Your CV will also be relatively short, especially when you are first applying for jobs. You may start with a single-page CV and build up to a two-page CV as you gain more knowledge and experience.

Chapters 5 to 7 will look in more detail at how to set out your CV and what to include in it.

CVs in this book

This book includes a number of CVs in different styles as examples of how you might approach writing your own CV. Please treat these as guidelines to follow and not as templates to copy: your CV should be written in your own words. There are no hard and fast rules about CVs, and you can adapt these examples to fit your own skills, experience and strengths. Also, please note that all names and career histories in these example CVs are fictitious and any resemblance to actual persons is purely coincidental.

Finally, the bulk of advice and CV examples in this book relate to applications for jobs in the United Kingdom. While it is not possible in a book of this length to cover all the various types and styles of CV used in other countries, Chapter 10: 'International CVs' does give some guidelines and resources to help you if you plan to apply to employers outside the United Kingdom.

Recording your life

What will you learn from this chapter?

This chapter covers recording your life and experience to date by gathering factual information on your education, work, skills and achievements. It also stresses the importance of making sure that this information is entered accurately on your CV.

The following two chapters cover **analysing yourself** (thinking about your skills and personality and how these fit with your career plans) and **researching employers** (identifying what they offer, whether they are right for you and what they will be looking for on your CV).

Get the facts right

Before you start to write your CV, you need to think about yourself, what you have done and how this can be used to show employers that you are a good candidate.

There are three stages to this process:

- Record your life – what you have done and when you have done it.
- Analyse yourself.
- Research the employer.

Why is this preparation important?

Having relevant information to hand will not only give you a resource to refer to quickly when completing applications (both CVs and application forms) but will also ensure that your CV is one hundred per cent accurate. This is important on a CV for two reasons:

Carelessness looks bad

Obvious errors in dates, names and so on can look careless, which is never a good impression to give on a CV.

Spot the mistakes!

Below is a list of some well-known companies: see if you can correct the common misspellings:

Macdonald's
Proctor & Gamble
Sainsburys
Addidas
Guiness
Vodaphone
Volkswagon
Glaxo Smith Klein
Lloyd's Bank

What is wrong with these extracts from students' CVs?

Education
University of Bristol, 2015 to date
Caxton School, 2009–2016

Work Experience
Sales Adviser, New Look, Swansea
June 2015–August 2014

(Answers are at the end of the chapter.)

Untruthfulness looks worse

Errors in grades, or any other information which could be regarded as misleading, could lead to a job offer being withdrawn if it is discovered. Even if you have genuinely made a mistake in stating a GCSE grade as a B instead of a C, and even if the actual grade would have made no difference to your application had it been correctly included, employers discover so many deliberate 'mistakes' of this sort that they will almost always assume the worst.

> In 2015, a legal employer checked a candidate's degree certificate, which showed that she had obtained a 2.2 rather than the 2.1 stated on her CV. The employer reported the applicant to the Solicitors Regulation Authority, which suspended her from practising law for 18 months and fined her £3000.

You might think that more minor misrepresentations, for example, extending your dates of employment to cover awkward gaps in your CV, are harmless, but the risk of getting found out is very real. In stressful situations such as job interviews, it's easy to forget what lies you've written on your CV!

An employer has a legal right to dismiss an employee for lying on a job application or CV. The employer will have hired that person, and entered into a contract with them, based on the information they provided. If some of the facts in that person's CV are untrue then the employee will have misled the employer and the contract will be considered invalid.

And even if the employer does not discover, or is willing to overlook, these 'inaccuracies', there are further potential problems to be faced:

> One candidate's CV for a prestigious graduate job in banking claimed that he was a proficient golfer. He got the job and was later invited to represent the bank at a City golfing event, only to perform spectacularly badly. This didn't put his job at risk, but it did mean that he lost a lot of respect among his colleagues and managers.

Draw up a career history/timeline

Put together key dates: when you started or left school and college, employment and so on.

You may find it helpful to produce a timeline such as this:

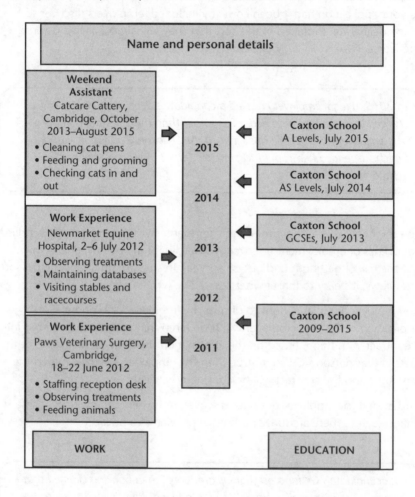

Alternatively, you could set out your education, work history, achievements, volunteering and so on, in a table:

Date	Event
September 2009	Started at Caxton School
18–22 June 2012	Work experience at Paws Veterinary Surgery
2–6 July 2012	Work experience at Newmarket Equine Hospital
July 2013	GCSEs
October 2013	Began weekend job at Catcare Cattery
July 2014	AS Levels
July 2015	A Levels

Gather information

Get together a folder with any certificates that you may need to refer to or show employers. These will mainly be exam certificates for A Levels and GCSEs or equivalent – you probably don't need to worry about your ten-metre swimming certificate.

Check details: for example, is the official name of your university 'Anytown University' or 'The University of Anytown'?

Think back over any work experience you have had so far. Note down information about it such as:

- What was the name of your employer?
- When did you start and finish employment there?
- What were your responsibilities?
- Who were you responsible to?
- Were you responsible for any other staff?
- What did you learn?
- What skills did you develop through this work?
- Did you make a difference? How?
- Did you receive any awards or commendations?

You don't need to be hyper-accurate in every detail – whether it was in April or May of your GCSE year that you gave up your paper round probably won't be really important – but this will help you to fit together your CV at the level of accuracy that will be expected.

Personal Development Planning

> *A structured and supported process undertaken by an individual to reflect upon their own learning, performance and/or achievement and to plan for their personal, educational and career development.*
>
> (Quality Assurance Agency for Higher Education 2009)

Your university may have a Personal Development Planning (PDP) tool that will help you to create and store records relating to your career and personal development. Do make use of this as early as possible, and keep it up to date. You can use it to gather, record and reflect on everything from academic assignments to work experience to extracurricular activities.

Personal Development Planning is more than just a record of factual details: you can also use it to note what you learned, and what skills you gained, from these experiences.

Recording information about activities you undertake at university, including academic work, extracurricular activities, prizes and employability awards, voluntary work and offices held in student union clubs and societies will help you to put together your Higher Education Achievement Report (HEAR). The HEAR is an extended academic transcript, now being introduced into many UK universities, which can be used, along with your degree certificate, to support your applications for employment and further study.

If your university uses HEAR, it will have examples of what a HEAR looks like, or see www.hear.ac.uk/about for a general overview.

The following example shows how you might record and analyse your experience and the skills you have developed through it:

Employer	Dates	Position	Responsibilities
Catcare Cattery, Cambridge	October 2013 – August 2015	Weekend Assistant	Cleaning cat pens Feeding and grooming cats Checking cats in and out

Skills Gained	Evidence
Communication	Greeting owners; answering owners' questions
Teamwork	Working with four colleagues; allocating tasks and working together to make sure these were completed on time
Attention to detail	Ensuring that cats on special diets received the right food; observing cats for changes in health or behaviour; checking vaccination certificates
Using initiative; lateral thinking	Finding ways to relate to cats and help them settle in
Patience	Always essential when working with cats!
Dedication and commitment	Started work at 7.00 a.m.

Interest	Dates	Activities involved
Fencing	From 2015	Joined University Fencing Club in Freshers' Week; attend training sessions and club events

Skills Gained	Evidence
• Learning new techniques • Quick responses • Safety awareness • Strategic thinking • Discipline and concentration	Achieved Bronze award in epée and foil at end of first term; working towards Silver

---

Exercise:

Now write your own plan using the one above as a starting point.

Now that you have gathered the factual information about what you have done, and the skills that you have gained through these activities, it is time to focus on these skills in more detail. The next chapter will help you to work out your key skills and how you can develop them further; Chapter 4: 'Researching Jobs and Employers' will look at relating these skills to jobs.

Answers to list of companies

All of these were spelt wrong! The correct spellings are below:

Wrong!	Correct!
Macdonald's	McDonald's
Proctor & Gamble	Procter & Gamble
Sainsburys	Sainsbury's
Addidas	Adidas
Guiness	Guinness
Vodaphone	Vodafone
Volkswagon	Volkswagen
Glaxo Smith Klein	GlaxoSmithKline
Lloyd's Bank	Lloyds Bank

Spot the mistakes!

1. Did this candidate really start university a year before they left school?
2. This time-travelling employee seems to have started work at New Look a year *after* they finished.

Finding out more

Cottrell, S. (2015) *Skills for Success: Personal Development and Employability*, 3rd edn (Basingstoke and New York: Palgrave).

Analysing yourself

Contents

What will you learn from this chapter?

Unless you know your skills, personality traits and achievements, it's difficult to write a good CV. A successful CV requires you to work out the skills required in the jobs you are applying for and to give concrete evidence of these skills. Writing a CV will help to clarify the way you see your skills, personality and achievements, and it will become clearer how to sell these to employers.

Analysing your skills

Exercise: analysing your skills

The following exercise will help you to identify which work-related skills you are strong in. Look at the following skills which are divided into categories such as Speaking. For each item, tick the box 'I have this skill' if you are competent at it, or 'I need to improve it' if you feel you are weak at it.

Skill	I have this skill	I need to improve it
Speaking: expressing your ideas clearly in speech		
Listening carefully to clarify and summarise what others are saying		
Being sensitive to body language as well as speech		
Making the right impression by making effective use of dress and speech		
Successfully speaking to an audience		
Teamwork: working confidently within a group		
Working cooperatively towards a common goal		
Contributing your own ideas effectively in groups and listening to others' opinions		
Taking a share of the responsibility		
Accepting and learning from constructive criticism and giving positive feedback		
Planning and Organising: able to plan and carry activities through effectively		
Managing your time effectively		
Setting priorities: most important/most urgent		
Action planning: identifying the steps needed to achieve your goals		
Working effectively to deadlines when under pressure		
Flexibility: adapting successfully to changing situations and environments		
Planning ahead but adapting goals in the light of changing situations		
Thinking quickly to respond to sudden changes in circumstances		
Taking a positive attitude to failure: persevering when things aren't working out		

Skill	I have this skill	I need to improve it
Using creativity/initiative in the generation of alternative solutions to a problem		
Persuading: convincing others, to discuss and reach agreement		
Putting your points across in a reasoned way		
Emphasising the positive aspects of your argument		
Understanding the needs of the other person		
Tactfully handling objections and making concessions to gain agreement		
Writing: being able to express yourself clearly in writing		
Gathering, analysing and arranging information logically		
Developing arguments in a logical way		
Condensing information: producing concise notes		
Adapting your writing style for different audiences		
Leadership: motivating and directing others		
Setting demanding but achievable goals		
Organising and motivating others/delegating tasks		
Making decisions and seeing them through		
Accepting responsibility for mistakes/bad decisions		
Investigating, Analysing and Problem Solving		
Gathering information systematically to establish facts and principles		
Analysing complex problems and identifying key factors		

Skill	I have this skill	I need to improve it
Clarifying the nature of a problem before acting		
Distinguishing between practical and impractical solutions		
Developing Professionalism: drive to achieve goals		
Accepting responsibility for your views and actions		
Being able to work under your own direction and initiative		
Paying care and attention to quality in your work		
Taking the opportunity to learn new skills		
SCORES: now give yourself one mark for each 'I have this skill' tick		

Skill	Score		Score
Speaking		Writing	
Teamwork		Leadership	
Planning and Organising		Investigating and Analysing	
Flexibility		Developing Professionalism	
Persuading			

Looking at the above results, what are your strongest skills? Do you agree with this analysis?

Exercise: think of examples of where you have used these skills

These examples could come from academic study, school, work or extracurricular activities. Here are some suggestions. Tick any that apply to you, and add any others which aren't listed below:

- ❏ Dealing tactfully with an angry customer in a shop job *(spoken communication and diplomacy)*
- ❏ Coaching junior players in a sports team *(leadership and motivating)*
- ❏ Producing a report *(writing)*
- ❏ Completing a group project for your course *(teamwork and organisation)*
- ❏ Helping to run a student society *(organising)*
- ❏ Fundraising for a charity *(persuading)*
- ❏ Acting as school prefect *(leadership, organising)*
- ❏ Being a course representative *(spoken communication and negotiating)*
- ❏ Becoming a student mentor *(listening, motivating)*
- ❏ Being a student ambassador *(persuading, leading)*
- ❏ Holding a part-time job whilst studying *(flexibility and time management)*
- ❏ Mending your bicycle or car *(problem solving and logical thinking)*
- ❏ Acting in a drama group *(teamwork and presentation skills)*
- ❏ Taking a summer internship *(developing professionalism)*
- ❏ Traveling round Europe on your own *(planning, independence)*
- ❏ Receiving the Duke of Edinburgh Award *(planning, determination)*
- ❏ Participating in Young Enterprise *(initiative, teamwork)*
- ❏ Writing for the university newspaper *(writing and creativity)*
- ❏ Volunteering *(helping, teamwork)*

Now choose three skills, and write down two examples of where you have demonstrated each skill.

Skill	Example 1	Example 2
1.		
2.		
3.		

The following skills map allows you to see these skills in relationship with one another.

Careers which might require evidence of core skills

Speaking	PR executive	Teacher	Speech therapist
Teamwork	Marketing manager	Nurse	Management consultant
Planning and organising	Events manager	Logistics manager	Retail manager
Flexibility	Social worker	Police officer	Journalist
Persuading	Advertising executive	Sales representative	Charity fundraiser
Writing	Solicitor	Publishing editor	Translator
Leadership	Armed forces officer	Retail manager	Production manager
Investigating	Computer analyst	Engineer	Research scientist
Developing Professionalism	Accountant	Lawyer	HR manager

Which careers might use your skills?

Write down some careers which might use your strongest skills and might interest you.

Developing your skills

Are there any skills that you are weak in which are important for the types of jobs you want? If so, work on developing these skills. A weakness in computing skills might be relatively easy to solve by online training, but others, such as persuading skills, might only be improved by practice.

Your personality

Your personality can strongly influence your choice of career. If you are not outgoing and independent, you may struggle in a sales career. A police officer has to be resilient, as does a TV producer – or anybody who commutes to work! Tact and sensitivity are particularly important for the helping careers, such as social work, but also help anybody who wants to get on with their colleagues.

Exercise: analysing your personality traits

Look at the following chart, and write down your three strongest personality traits. If you have other traits which are not in the chart, feel free to use these instead. For each trait, give at least one example of where you have used it.

```
                              Independent        Proactive
               Enterprising
                          Resilient  Quick-thinking  Energetic   Ambitious
      Resourceful                                              Assertive
                          Determined   Courageous   Enthusiastic
      Versatile
                                                              Confident
  Intelligent          [ Creative ]          [ Outgoing ]
                                                              Positive
     Focused
                       [ Your Personality ]          Cheerful
                                            Cooperative
     Practical
                                                              Sociable
      Precise          [ Logical ]          [ Caring ]
                                                              Understanding
    Meticulous
                  Analytical    Calm     Loyal   Tactful
      Organised                Cautious         Polite     Sensitive
                Efficient              Mature   Patient
                          Reliable   Honest
```

Personality trait	Example of where you've used it

These traits could provide useful material for your covering letter or CV profile.

But I'm not outgoing!

Many students feel that they haven't done a lot in life and so don't have a lot to offer, but many traits which you may feel are unimportant are highly valued by employers.

Introversion is often seen as a negative trait, but Charles Darwin, Abraham Lincoln, Mahatma Ghandi, Nelson Mandela, Audrey Hepburn, Alfred Hitchcock, Clint Eastwood, Albert Einstein, Henry Ford, J.K. Rowling, Isaac Newton and Barack Obama were/are all introverts! Introverts tend to have a few deep friendships rather than many superficial relationships. They tend to have good judgment[1] and are often careful thinkers, good at *solving problems* and considering all the consequences when making decisions, which allows them to assess risks more effectively.

Surprisingly, the best predictor of future job performance and satisfaction is not leadership or communication skills; it is in fact, conscientiousness,[2] which is linked to better motivation and task completion and also with work satisfaction. Conscientious individuals usually have strong self-control.

They are responsible, diligent and usually somewhat cautious and slow to act. They tend to plan in advance and concentrate on achieving their aims, focusing on goals and following things through to completion. They are often well organised, purposeful and determined.

Your achievements

An achievements section in your CV shows you can get things done: that you are someone who goes above and beyond the norm. Achievements have more power than tasks and duties. Some students feel that spelling out their achievements is boasting, but this isn't true if you back up your achievements with evidence.

It took me a long time to write my CV because I wanted to get it just right. I first analysed and mapped out my skills and achievements and thought about how to showcase these. Writing the CV helped me to evaluate my strengths and how best to demonstrate these to employers. I now feel more confident when applying for jobs and have a better idea about what careers might suit my abilities.

Supreet, a science graduate

Exercise: brainstorm your achievements

Get a large, blank sheet of paper, and write down any achievements that you can think of, even if these seem insignificant. Achievements could come from your education, work or interests. You can use the following examples of types of achievements to stimulate ideas. Keep going until you completely run out of ideas; then cull any weak ones.

Not every student will have high-level achievements, and it's fine to mention achievements that are more day-to-day, such as getting a high grade in a project or dissertation, acting in a school play, being accomplished at playing a musical instrument, producing publicity materials for a student society or working as a waiter and getting commended by customers.

Here are some examples to get you started. A good way to present your achievements is in a bulleted list, starting with an action word (as shown in bold in the example). Using action words at the start of bullet points gives them impact.

Type of achievement	Example with action word in bold
Succeeded at a challenge	**Successfully completed** Gold Duke of Edinburgh Award, including a demanding five-day expedition in the Alps
Solved a problem	**Designed** flyers for my student society, which raised membership by 40 per cent
Excelled at a task	**Scored** 75 per cent in the National Mathematics Olympiad **Graduated** in top 5 per cent of my class
Added value	**Significantly raised** customer satisfaction by providing high levels of service
Had an idea which was successfully implemented or created something	**Started up** the university debating society, including promoting the society, gaining funding, planning a programme and motivating new members
Improved service to customers	**Trained** six new staff in procedures to increase quality of customer service
Saved or raised money or saved time or resources	**Successfully completed** a half marathon which raised £500 for charity
Increased sales, profits or clients	**Consistently exceeded** sales targets and was awarded prize for sales assistant of the year
Showed leadership	**Led** my final year group project, which achieved a grade of 78 per cent
Improved efficiency	**Developed** a spreadsheet which increased efficiency for a company
Went the extra mile to help	**Commended** by supervisors for consistently meeting deadlines and dealing effectively with demanding clients
Won a prize, award or competition	**Awarded** trophy for 'Most Improved Football Player' in university team
Elected or nominated for something	**Nominated** for course representative, where I worked closely with staff and students to successfully resolve problems

Type of achievement	Example with action word in bold
Leadership	**Presented** talks as Head Girl, promoting the school to large audiences of parents
Planning and organising	**Planned** and organised a successful freshers' event for 300 students
Learned a skill	**Developed** time management skills by successfully coping with a degree, part-time job and active social life
Gained a promotion	**Promoted** from assistant to supervisor in part-time job

Exercise: write about your achievements

- **What achievements could you add to your CV?** Use the list above to give you ideas. What did you improve, discover or create?
- **What did you do?** If it was a problem, what was your solution to it? What was your personal involvement?
- **What was the outcome?** What difference did you make? What have you changed? Give specific and measurable examples where possible, e.g. increased membership by 30 per cent.

List your achievements below:

_____

_____

_____

_____

Cultural fit

Cultural fit deals with how you will fit in with the culture of the organisation you wish to work for. Employers want graduates whose values, beliefs, outlook and behaviour fit in with the organisation's culture, as this will enable them to thrive. A graduate who works well in a team should work well in an organisation that stresses cooperation, whereas someone who likes to work alone may not fit in. Someone who likes to be told what to do will struggle in a company that stresses staff empowerment and personal accountability. An authoritarian manager won't be successful in a company with a relaxed management style.

> One student applied to an accountancy firm and was surprised to be asked a lot of questions about the sporting achievements he had included in his CV. He later found out that nearly everyone in the firm played for one of the firm's various teams and that sport played a large part in the firm's culture.

What traits do you have that are important to employers?

What role do you typically play in a team?	
Leader: coordinates and directs the team	**Ideas person:** creative individual who suggests new ways to do things
Encourager: supports and praises team members to keep motivation high	**Compromiser:** maintains harmony in the group by resolving conflict
Clarifier: summarises the team's discussions and conclusions. Clarifies group objectives and keeps the group focussed	**Analyst:** logical, objective types who offer critical analysis. Slow in coming to a decision and good at evaluating competing proposals

Give an example of where you have demonstrated this role:

What is your leadership style?	
Authoritarian leaders tell their team what they want done and how, without asking for advice.	**Procedural leaders** work 'by the book', precisely following procedures.
Transformational leaders inspire their team with their vision. They supply the goal but allow members to choose their way of reaching it.	**Participative leaders** build consensus through participation: the leader makes the final decision, but the team to contribute to the process.

Laissez-faire leaders allow team members to make the decisions. The team makes its own decisions which are then approved by the leader.

Give an example of where you have used this style:

Other attributes	Answer below
Do you prefer working alone or in a team?	
Do you make **decisions** quickly or agonise over them? Do you tend to use logic and analysis or gut feelings and intuition?	
Are you **detail-orientated** or do you prefer the bigger picture?	
Do you prefer **starting or finishing** projects?	
When **planning and organising** tasks, do you prefer a structured or informal approach?	
Do you enjoy doing **routine** tasks, or do you get bored quickly?	
How do you handle conflict? Meekly give in? Act aggressively? Negotiate a solution?	
Can you persuade and influence people?	
How do you cope under **pressure?**	
Are you resilient? How do you cope with failure? Do you bounce back quickly? Learn from your mistakes? Try other methods?	
Are you **adaptable:** do you cope well with change and uncertainty?	
Do you enjoy **meeting new people**, or do you find this rather stressful?	
Do you show **professionalism?** Do you have a quality orientation and take pride in your work – for example no spelling mistakes in your CV!	

Are you **reliable?** Can you meet targets consistently and take on extra tasks as needed?	
Do you **learn new things quickly?**	
Do you have **energy and enthusiasm?**	
Do people think you are honest and **have integrity?**	

Finding out more

For more about how to sell your skills and cultural fit, see *'Excel at Graduate Interviews'* in this series of Palgrave Career Skills books.

References

1. Helgoe, L. (2010), 'Revenge of the Introvert', *Psychology Today*, www.psychologytoday.com/articles/201009/revenge-the-introvert.
2. Barrick, M., and Mount, M. (1993), 'Autonomy as a Moderator of the Relationships between the Big Five Personality Dimensions and Job Performance', *Journal of Applied Psychology*, 78(1): 111–18.

Chapter 4

Researching jobs and employers

What will you learn from this chapter?

You will learn how to research employers and jobs and where to find the information that you need to prepare a targeted CV. The chapter explains how jobs are advertised and how employers draw up job descriptions and person specifications that set out what they are looking for in candidates. This information will help you to read job advertisements, understand employers' requirements and adapt your CV for different jobs.

Why do this research?

You need to present yourself as the ideal candidate – but what makes the ideal candidate in the employer's eyes? Researching the job, and gathering information about the employer, will help you to find this out and match yourself to what they want. You can then use this information to prepare a CV that will impress the employer by showing them clearly that you understand the job and have the skills that it requires.

Equally importantly, doing this research means that you will be able to apply for jobs and employers that you are confident will fit well with your strengths and interests and therefore offer you job satisfaction.

Researching job roles

What you need to know about jobs

- What does the job involve? You may think that you know, but your idea may be inaccurate or incomplete. Researching the job will help you to avoid false stereotypes such as 'accountants sit at a desk and add up figures' or 'human resources managers are there to help employees with their personal problems'.
- What skills, qualifications and/or experience does the job require? Do you already have them? If not, how can you develop them?
- Which employers might offer this job? Again, there may be unexpected answers to this question. Lawyers do not just work in law firms; librarians work in business and specialist libraries as well as universities and public libraries and IT specialists are much in demand in finance and manufacturing.
- What practical issues might you need to take into account? Is this a job that you could do almost anywhere, or will you need to relocate or commute? What are the working hours likely to be? What sort of environment might you work in? What is the salary level?

Where to find information

Start with career sites for students and graduates, such as Prospects and TARGETjobs. Both these sites have job profiles/job descriptions which outline key points such as:

- The responsibilities of the job: what would you be doing and what does it involve?
- Skills needed to succeed in this job.
- Typical employers.
- Getting in: qualifications and work experience.
- Career prospects: how your career might develop.

Professional bodies, such as the Law Society or the Institute of Physics, can provide general information on job roles and qualifications in their field.

You can use job advertisements to find out more background to jobs – even ones that you may not yet be able to apply for, or that are in the wrong part of the country for you. A job ad that provides a good job description and person specification (see below) can be an invaluable source of information that you can use to apply for similar jobs with other employers. Even if the ad asks for more experience than you can offer, it could help you to learn what type of experience would be helpful to set you on track.

Researching employers

What you need to know about employers

- What does the organisation do? What products does it make? What services does it provide? Who are its clients?
- Who owns it? Who does it own? What other organisations are associated with it?
- What significant events have occurred in recent months, such as mergers/takeovers, changes in senior management, expansion, new product lines?
- Are there any key trends and events in the wider business environment, such as new legislation, that may have an impact on its activities? What innovations have competitors made?
- What roles does it recruit for, and what career paths does it offer? How many past graduate recruits are still with the organisation, and how have their careers developed?
- What makes the organisation different from its competitors? What are its key selling points and how does it present itself to candidates and customers?
- What is the organisational culture like? As we saw in Chapter 3, finding an employer that fits your work style and values will help you to fit in and find your work motivating and satisfying.

Where to find information

- The organisation's own website. Don't just look at the 'Recruitment' or 'Graduate' pages but explore other sections, in particular those aimed at clients, shareholders and the media: this is where you can pick up the latest news and information.
- Graduate job sites such as Prospects, Target and Rate My Placement. These have employer profiles that give an outline of the organisation, its graduate recruitment and feedback from current graduates/interns.
- Social media. Most major organisations will have a wide social media presence: not just Facebook and Twitter but including YouTube, Instagram, Buzzfeed and blogs. You can also use LinkedIn to find

people working at the company, get an idea of their job role and career development and maybe even make contact with them.

- News media. You don't have to get to grips with the Financial Times: the business news pages of the BBC, Guardian, Independent and Telegraph are all clear, straightforward and free to use. You can search them to find any recent news items relating to an employer that interests you.

- Networking. Use employer events and careers fairs, at your university or at national level, alumni networks and university careers services to make contacts with graduate recruiters.

Is it worth all the effort?

Yes, yes and yes. Researching jobs does take time and effort, but it is better to spend several hours on one well-researched application than to spend the same amount of time on a dozen standard and unfocused applications. It can be tempting to skip this stage when you have to combine job hunting with your studies, or when a deadline is imminent, but taking time to do your research will not only improve your application – it will show the employer that you are motivated and genuinely interested in working for them.

How jobs are advertised

Most large organisations will, before drawing up a job advert, go through a number of steps designed to give both recruitment staff and potential applicants a good understanding of the job and what it involves. Doing this means that candidates can be more confident that the job is right for them and employers will find it easier to ascertain this from applications.

The first thing an employer needs to do is define the job by carrying out a **job analysis**. What tasks does this post involve? What qualifications, transferable and practical skills are needed? Who does the job holder work with – in their own department, in other parts of the company and externally? Even if the employer is recruiting to fill a vacancy created by someone leaving, this gives them an opportunity to review the role, to look at the strengths of the previous employee and at anything that the new member of staff might offer to enhance the job and the organisation.

This analysis will then be used to draw up a **job description (JD)**. which is used as the basis of the job advert. The JD sets out the purpose of the role, key tasks and responsibilities and other factors such as location, salary and who the job holder will report to.

A job description may also include an outline of the skills, experience, competencies and qualifications required to perform well in the job; however, this information really belongs in the **person specification (PS)**.

The person specification is often divided into 'essential' and 'desirable' attributes, as in the following example:

Job title: Summer Retail Assistant
Employer: A heritage property and tourist attraction
Location: Central London

Requirements	Essential	Desirable
Education and training		
GCSE Maths or equivalent	✓	
Experience		
Previous customer service experience		✓
Experience of cash handling and using electronic tills		✓
Personal Skills		
Excellent verbal communication skills	✓	
A friendly, helpful and positive attitude	✓	
Good team player	✓	
Able to work well under pressure	✓	
Reliable and trustworthy	✓	
Additional requirements		
Knowledge of a language other than English		✓

Targeting your CV

Your CV should demonstrate as many of the key skills, experience or personal qualities set out in the PS as possible.

Remember that recruiters will have a large number of CVs to read in a short time and will not be willing to put any extra effort into interpreting your CV: you need to show them, as briefly and clearly as possible, that you fit their picture of the ideal candidate. Don't just **tell them** that you have the skills/experience or qualities that they are looking for, but **show them**.

For example, a good CV for the Summer Retail Assistant job on the previous page, would demonstrate the 'essential' skills through headings and information such as these:

RELEVANT EXPERIENCE[1]

University Student Union 2014–2016

- Worked in a team[2] of six in a busy[3] student entertainment venue.
- Took food orders,[4] served drinks and ensured that customers had an enjoyable experience.[5]
- Used electronic tills[6] to take payments; cashed up at the end of each shift.[7]
- Flexibility was important to support colleagues[8] and handle any problems that arose.

Notes on the above 'Relevant Experience' section

---

1. Placing your most relevant experience under this heading, rather than listing all your experience in one big section, makes it stand out.
2. Good team player.
3. Able to work well under pressure.
4. Communication skills.
5. Friendly and positive.
6. Experience of cash handling and using electronic tills.
7. Reliable and trustworthy.
8. Helpful.

Reading job adverts

You may not always have a detailed JD and PS, especially if you are applying through a jobs board or recruitment agency. Sometimes, all that you have to go on will be a short paragraph such as:

We are looking for high calibre graduates (2.1 or above) to pursue a career in accounting and finance. The environment is fast paced but offers full support in a friendly setting to become a qualified Chartered Accountant. You will be offered a competitive salary with a clear path to progression and career development.

To apply for the role you must be proactive in your approach to your career and be able to manage your time effectively.

Although this advert gives very little detail, phrases such as 'fast-paced' and 'progression and career development' give clues as to what the job requires and the type of candidates that the employer is looking for. This is confirmed by the requirement that you should be proactive and a good time manager. You can use this information to adapt your CV and covering letter to highlight times when you have worked independently, managed your time effectively, taken responsibility and shown ambition.

RELEVANT EXPERIENCE

University Student Union 2014–2016

- Worked in a team of six in a busy student entertainment venue.
- Used electronic tills to take payments; cashed up at the end of each shift.
- Flexibility was important to support colleagues and handle any problems that arose.
- Suggested new items for the menu, one of which became a best-seller.
- Undertook extra training and was promoted to a supervisory role after six months, with responsibility for organising shifts and special events.

As well as the skills noted earlier, this adapted version also shows that the candidate is proactive (they have made successful innovations); ambitious (undertaking extra training and achieving promotion); able to take responsibility (having carried out a supervisory role) and able to manage their own time and that of others (organising shifts and events).

For this job role, you could also use more general information on the role of a chartered accountant, produced by professional bodies and sites such as Prospects and TARGETJobs, to help you find out what other skills are important in the work. This CV shows some of these other skills relevant to accountancy, such as teamwork and numeracy.

What if there isn't a job advert?

Sometimes you may be applying for a job that hasn't been advertised – you may not even know if it exists!

This can happen when:

- You are making a speculative approach to find out if an employer has any job opportunities.
- You have been invited to send your CV to a contact.
- You are sending your CV to a recruitment agency.

Don't panic – you can still do your research, using the resources suggested under 'Researching Job Roles' earlier in this chapter. This will allow you to get a general idea of what job roles the employer might offer and what they would involve. Being clear and realistic in what you are asking for, and showing your knowledge of the employer and/or the sector they work in, will get you off to a good start and show the employer that you are a serious and motivated candidate. This research will also help you to ask the right questions at an interview.

Finding out more

Prospects (2016) *Job Profiles*, www.prospects.ac.uk/job-profiles.
TARGETJobs (2016) *Job Descriptions*, https://targetjobs.co.uk/careers-advice/job-descriptions.

Both Prospects and TARGETJobs are major national careers sites which provide job profiles/job descriptions outlining what the work involves; skills and qualifications needed; typical employers; links to professional bodies and where to look for vacancies. They also have profiles of many large graduate recruiters, some of which include tips on the application and interview process.

Rate My Placement, www.ratemyplacement.co.uk.

Rate My Placement focuses on placement years and summer internships, reviewed by students who have had this experience.

Barnett, B. (2012) 'When Choosing a Job, Culture Matters', *Harvard Business Review blog*, https://hbr.org/2012/05/when-choosing-a-job-culture-ma.

Rook, S. (2013) *The Graduate Career Guidebook* (Basingstoke and New York: Palgrave Macmillan).

Types of CV

Contents

What will you learn from this chapter?

You will learn about the different styles of CV, how to set them out and how to decide which works best for you.

Introduction

There is no one 'best' or 'right' way to set out a CV. Remember that your CV is not a list of everything you have ever done: it is a marketing document. This means that it needs to demonstrate your skills and achievements to an employer in a way that clearly shows what you have to offer and relates that to the organisation and to the job. The 'best' way to set out a CV is the way that shows you off to the best advantage and will persuade an employer that you are worth interviewing!

There are three main ways to set out your CV: chronological, skills-based or hybrid. Any of these formats may be set out over one or two pages (see Chapter 7: 'Making Your CV Look Good').

The following pages show you how you might set out a CV in each of these styles, with examples.

Chronological CVs

Chronology refers to arranging events in the order of their occurrence in time. Strictly speaking, a CV should be 'reverse chronological', starting with what you are doing now (or have done most recently) and working backwards. Since your most recent experience is likely to be most relevant, this will sell you to the best advantage.

A chronological CV is divided into sections, such as 'Education' and 'Work Experience', that set out what you have done in those categories, when and where you did it. Usually, chronological CVs also include sections such as 'Skills' and 'Interests'.

A chronological CV works well for:

- people without a large amount of experience;
- people with a fairly straightforward career path;
- people whose education and experience relate closely to the job they are applying for.

It works less well for:

- people with a mixture of experience, most of which is not relevant;
- career changers – people with a lot of experience in an area they are now trying to move away from and which may cause them to be pigeonholed;
- people with gaps in their career history due to illness, childcare and so on.

Nina Patel

33 Union Street, Manchester, M6 3AE

Phone: 0161 496 0744   Email: nina-patel-33@gmail.com

EDUCATION

University of Essex, BSc (Hons) Computer Science, 2014 to date
Obtained 62% in my second-year exams, equivalent to a 2:1
Modules include:

Software Engineering	Compiling Techniques	Computer Networks
Digital Systems	Operating Systems	Database Systems

Project: Development of a Linux-based network system. Achieved 70%

Salford Community College, 2012–2014
A Levels: Mathematics B, Physics C **AS Levels:** Biology C, Chemistry D

St John's School, Manchester, 2007–2012
8 GCSEs at grades A and B including Mathematics, English and French

WORK EXPERIENCE

Assistant, The Raj Restaurant, Salford, summer 2015

- As the main connection between chef and customers, I managed orders and ensured every customer was happy.
- Front of house organisation, greeting customers and managing reservations in a smooth and efficient manner.

Customer Service Assistant, Next, Salford, summer 2014
Served customers, answered queries, managed stock and resolved problems. This involved anticipating customers' needs, dealing with unexpected situations and working under pressure.

Interests and Achievements

- Elected as Secretary of the Indian Society.
- Organised a charity fun run for Rag Week, raising £350.
- Play for the University hockey team.

SKILLS

- Linux; Windows 8.1; Java; VB.Net and Python.
- Good knowledge of MS Word, PowerPoint and Excel.
- Full, clean driving licence.

1
2
3
4
5
6
7
8
9
10

This is a simple, one-page chronological CV which Nina Patel could use to apply for internships, placements or graduate jobs relevant to her degree.

1. Head your CV with your name, in a large font size to stand out.
2. You don't need the words 'Curriculum Vitae', 'Name' or 'Address' – it's obvious what these are!
3. Putting your email and phone number on the same line saves space and makes your CV symmetrical.
4. Dates should be in reverse chronological order, with the most recent first.
5. Include modules and projects if relevant to the job you are applying for. Employers in the IT sector would know what these modules cover and would expect Nina to provide this level of detail about her degree.
6. Names of schools and employers in bold, to stand out.
7. Nina summarises her GCSEs to save space.
8. Subheadings should be in identical fonts and sizes. Larger size fonts help these to stand out.
9. Evidence of transferable skills.
10. Don't just say 'Good computing skills', but give details of specific programs and packages that you can use. Note the spelling of 'PowerPoint'.

This CV can be adapted to apply for different jobs, for example by changing the order, or the amount of detail in different sections. The example on the next page is still chronological, but in this CV Nina puts her work experience before her studies as this is more likely to be relevant to the retail employers she is targeting for part-time or vacation work. She also leaves out some of her more specialised computer skills and adds others to focus on those most relevant to retail and customer service.

Nina Patel

33 Union Street, Manchester, M6 3AE
Phone: 0161 496 0744   Email: nina-patel-33@gmail.com

A positive, enthusiastic student with varied customer service experience, seeking part-time work during university term-times

WORK EXPERIENCE

Assistant, The Raj Restaurant, Salford, summer 2015

- As the main connection between chef and customers, I managed orders and ensured every customer was happy.
- Front of the house organisation, greeting customers and managing reservations in a smooth and efficient manner.

Customer Service Assistant, Next, Salford, summer 2014

- Served customers, answered queries, managed stock and resolved problems.
- This involved anticipating customers' needs, dealing with unexpected situations and working under pressure to provide an excellent service.

EDUCATION AND QUALIFICATIONS

The University of Essex, BSc Computer Science 2014–2017

Salford Community College, 2012–2014

A Levels: Mathematics B, Physics C **AS Levels:** Biology C, Chemistry D

St John's School, Manchester, 2007–2012
8 GCSEs at grades A and B, including Mathematics, English and French.

SKILLS

- Experience of using electronic point of sale and booking systems
- Good knowledge of MS Word, PowerPoint and Excel
- Full, clean driving licence

References available on request

Tips for chronological CVs

1. Don't feel you need to include everything you have done – you can summarise if you have had lots of different jobs.
2. Don't go too far back in time – there is no need to include your primary school or playing for the under-tens football team.
3. Don't leave long gaps of time without explaining them in some way – see Chapter 13: 'Mind the Gap - and other CV problems' for advice on dealing with any gaps.
4. Remember that a CV is not just a list of everything you have done. Even on a chronological CV, you can often work examples of your skills into your work experience or extracurricular activities, or include an 'Achievements' section;
5. Check your dates and make sure they are accurate.

One candidate included a section headed 'Achievements' which began with:

- Year Two 'Bookworm' Award for Best Reader
- Prizes for 100% attendance in Years 2, 3, 5 and 6
- Cub Scout Personal Challenge Award

This went on for a full page until they reached 'Clean provisional driving licence', although the employer had long given up on the CV by that time!

Skills-based CVs

If you find that your life and career to date make it difficult to set out a chronological CV, this approach is likely to work better for you. It emphasises the skills you have gained through all aspects of your life and only gives brief, factual details of education, employment and so on.

The skills highlighted in this type of CV are **transferable skills**: those which can be used in different settings. Showing an employer, for example, that you have demonstrated teamworking skills in university project groups and sports suggests that you will easily be able to fit into a team in the workplace.

What should a skills-based CV include?

- Key skills: those set out in the job description/person specification
- Evidence that you have used these skills. This can be from any aspect of your life:
  - Education.
  - Employment and other work experience.
  - Extracurricular activities.
  - Volunteering.
  - Your personal life, such as family or caring responsibilities.
- Brief factual details of your education and employment. If you don't include these, employers may think you are trying to be evasive or hide something.
- The usual personal and contact details.

Tips for a good skills-based CV

- Relate the skills to the job.
- Give examples of how and where you have shown these skills.
- Try to pick your examples from a range of different activities, such as work, study and extracurricular activities. This shows your versatility.
- Don't give too many examples and keep them brief. Two or three bullet points should be fine.
- You can include practical skills, such as IT and language skills, in your list as well as transferable skills.

Skills-based CVs are not just for mature graduates or career changers! Anyone can use this style of CV to show an employer what you can offer in relation to the job. Many application forms for graduate jobs take a skills-based approach so this is equally acceptable to use in your CV.

A skills-based CV needs to be based around the skills that are most important to the employer. These will be set out in the job description or job advertisement (see Chapter 4: 'Researching Jobs and Employers').

The example skills-based CV on the following pages has been structured in response to this job advertisement:

We are recruiting an intern to plan, run and market events at universities around the country. You should have experience of events organising, social media and budgeting, and be competent in research and report writing, with a knowledge of Excel and PowerPoint. The job will involve regular public speaking, so confidence and good presentation skills are essential.

Donna Draper

23 Lords Avenue, Malmesbury, Wiltshire, MM25 9AL
donna0708draper@gmail.com   07700 900011
https://uk.linkedin.com/donnakldraper123

SKILLS

Organising
- As president of UWE RAG, organised over 20 fundraising events during my year of office, raising £2400.
- Supervised a team of 20 part-time staff in a busy city centre pub, organising rotas and briefing the team on new products and promotions.
- As a postgraduate student, managed my time between study, research, part-time work and extracurricular activities.

Public Speaking
- Attended Model UN conference in Brussels, taking part in debates as the representative for Brazil.
- Stood for election to student union as campus rep, presenting my manifesto at hustings.
- Taught English to groups of children aged from 7 to 11 at summer language schools.

Research and writing
- Researched and approached sponsors for RAG events.
- Produced a 10,000-word Master's degree dissertation.
- Produced a report for the SocPol Research think tank on the role of volunteers and support groups at hospitals within an NHS Trust.

Social media
- Author of two blogs, www.lifeasapostgrad.com on student experiences and www.roundmyway.net on local environmental issues.

- As communications officer of the Environment and Conservation Society at UWE, set up Facebook, Twitter and Instagram accounts to raise awareness of events and issues. These achieved over 700 followers.

Budgeting

- Worked closely with the RAG treasurer to monitor budgets and spending on events and to draft proposals to potential sponsors.

IT Skills

- Proficient in Excel, PowerPoint and other MS Office packages (ECDL).

EDUCATION AND QUALIFICATIONS

Bangor University, MA Social Policy 2015–2016

Covered research design, data collection and analysis, policy research and evaluation, applied social research.
Dissertation on the influence of local government policies on the integration of students into the local community.

UWE, Bristol, BA Politics and International Relations, First Class Honours, 2012–2015

WORK EXPERIENCE

- Bar Person, Y Dafarn Newydd, Bangor, 2015–2016
- Bar Supervisor, The Green Lion, Bristol, 2013–2015
- Intern, SocPol Research, London SW1, July 2014
- Telephone Fundraiser, Development Office, UWE, March 2014
- English Language Teacher, Buckingham House School of English, Summer 2013
- Volunteer at various charity and community events, including fun runs, street collections and working parties at nature reserves.

POSTS OF RESPONSIBILITY

- President of UWE RAG
- Media officer of UWE Environment and Conservation Society
- Course rep for MA Social Policy students at Bangor

INTERESTS

- Writing for www.lifeasapostgrad.com/ and www.roundmyway.net/
- Play for a local pub rounders team
- Running: currently training for a half-marathon

References available on request

Donna's CV is closely tailored to the job description, using words and phrases from it, such as 'organising', 'social media' and 'budgeting' as headings in her CV. She gives a diverse range of examples of these skills: for example, she does not just rely on the research skills gained through her master's degree but also shows that she has carried out different types of research outside academia, for RAG and the think tank.

On a skills-based CV, you don't need to give very much detail about your past employment or extracurricular activities. All the key information from these should have been included in your skills outline, meaning that you just need to list employers, job titles and dates.

Make sure that the examples of skills that you give will help your CV: the ones below won't!

- **Languages:** No foreign languages but fluent English *(we can all speak at least one language!).*
- **Negotiation:** I always win arguments with my girlfriend.
- **IT skills:** Regularly use a laptop.
- **Communication:** I talk to people almost every day.
- **Leadership:** Trained my dog to walk to heel.
- I can pick up almost anything with my toes.

Hybrid CVs

A hybrid CV allows you to get the best of both worlds: setting out your chronological education and employment history but also having a short section to highlight your most relevant skills and/or experience.

This section should come at the beginning: like a personal profile (see Chapter 6: 'What Should Your CV Include?'), it will act as a 'headline' to catch the reader's attention, give them key information and make them want to read on.

The remainder of the CV is then likely to take a chronological approach. As with a 'pure' chronological CV, you can include examples and evidence of your skills when describing your education and work experience, but try to avoid repetition.

The skills you note may come from study, work experience, volunteering or extracurricular activities: an advantage of this approach is that you can pull together relevant experience across several different activities and bring it to the reader's attention from the start.

Like chronological CVs, hybrid CVs may not work so well for people with a diverse career history, as they still focus mainly on your experience.

Tips for a good hybrid CV

- Keep the skills section brief – four or five bullet points.
- As previously, relate the skills to the job and provide evidence – examples of how and where you have shown these skills.

The two example CVs on the following pages show how skills sections can be incorporated into a chronological CV to produce a hybrid CV that highlights your skills as well as your experience.

William Lo Man Li

78 Harbour Street, King's Lynn, Norfolk, NR26 3KD
will-lo-man-li@yahoo.com   07700 900011

PROFILE

A graduate with extensive and varied experience in retail and sales, seeking to join a sales
management training programme in the motor industry.

1

SKILLS

- A wide range of sales experience in retail, telesales and customer service
- A strong leader as well as a supportive team player

2

- Enjoy helping people: able to listen well and always willing to go the extra mile to provide
  customer satisfaction
- Excellent numeracy and verbal/written communication skills
- Proficient in the use of spreadsheets and databases
- Willing to work hard with a proven track record of meeting and exceeding targets

EDUCATION

University of Nottingham, BSc Management   2013 – 2016

Modules included Managing Service Operations; Entrepreneurship & Business; Organisational
Behaviour

3

King's Lynn High School   2007 – 2012

A Levels: Business (A), Psychology (A), History (C)
GCSEs: 11 at grades A–C including Maths (A) and English Language (A)

WORK EXPERIENCE

Enterprise Rent-a-Car – Summer Intern   June – August 2015

- Working in a small team and learning all aspects of the car rental business
- Liaising with individual and corporate customers both face-to-face and on the phone
- Handling documentation for car rentals and ensuring this was completed accurately and
  understood by the customer

4

- A wide variety of responsibilities including finance, operational management and marketing

E-Phone Mobile Networks – Telesales Adviser 2015 to date   5

- Contacted customers to advise on new products and services and to generate upgrades
- Met and exceeded minimum call rate and sales targets
- Used my communication skills and product knowledge to build a rapport with customers
- This role enabled me to understand the psychology of selling products and customer needs in order to find the appropriate product

Madison Menswear, Norwich – Assistant Manager   2012 – 2013   6

- Managed a staff of eight in a sales-driven environment; responsible for planning work shifts and holidays
- Monitored individual staff performance and allocated targets
- Checked tills, cashed up and banked takings
- Responsible for handling customer queries, problems and complaints
- Flexibility was essential to inspire and motivate staff and ensure customer satisfaction.

H & M, Norwich – Sales Assistant   2011 – 2012

- Sold clothing and accessories and gave advice to customers during the busy Christmas and New Year period
- Gained experience in customer services in a sales-driven environment
- Met and exceeded sales targets
- Due to my performance and teamwork my contract was extended for a further six months.

INTERESTS   7

- Secretary of University Car Club, organising and promoting events and liaising with car manufacturers, dealers and motorsport organisers
- Car maintenance: I have restored two 1970s Minis and am currently working on a 1979 MGB GT. As a member of the Mini and MG Owners' Clubs, I attend events to meet fellow enthusiasts and share knowledge
- Play five-a-side football regularly with friends
- Avid follower of motorsports, attending the British Grand Prix whenever possible as well as rallies and touring car events

Adebayo Akinwande

42 Quark Street, Sunderland, SR2 7NW
Email: ade97@akinwande.net   **Mobile:** 07700 900370

EDUCATION

2013–2016 Northumbria University, BSc Astrophysics (2.1)

Subjects Included:

Astrophysics	Quantum mechanics	Thermal physics
Nuclear physics	Exoplanets	Image processing
Problem solving	Spacecraft design	Stars and galaxies
Mathematics	Solid state physics	Space science
Medical physics	Relativity	Nuclear physics

Practical Skills Gained during my Degree

- Gained experience working with others and learning hands-on the properties of metal, magnetic fields, electric fields and the electromagnetic spectrum, most notably light
- Learned how to carry out experiments with accuracy, analyse the results and draw conclusions
- Learned new mathematical techniques, such as calculus, and used them to solve real-world problems, including quantum mechanical, thermal and statistical problems

2006–2013 Wearside College, Sunderland

BTEC National in Science and Engineering: DDD (Distinction)

GCSEs: 10, including Maths, English and Science from A to C

OTHER SKILLS

Team Work

- Played for University American Football team and took on responsibility for kit management
- Worked on degree projects within small groups of students
- In retail, have worked both in a team and as team leader

1

Communication   2

- Verbal communication skills used in delivering presentations and in helping customers
- Writing skills developed through producing assignments, posters, essays and projects for my degree

Problem solving

- Continuous problem-solving exercises given as assessments, which frequently required mathematical analysis and evaluation

IT Skills: Competent in MS Office packages, C++, LATeX and Python

WORK EXPERIENCE

Student Union Shop, Northumbria University (2012–2013)

- Began as a casual member of staff, operating tills and filling shelves
- Promoted within a year to a supervisor role, where I was relied on to create orders, check in and organise stock, cash up tills, date checks, and deal with customer complaints
- Also had responsibility for staff management, including drawing up rotas, prioritising jobs and conducting staff appraisals

Morrison's Supermarket, Sunderland (2010–2012)

- Assistant in various departments including checkouts, delicatessen and coffee shop
- Responsibilities included serving customers, preparing food and maintaining hygiene and   3
  product quality

INTERESTS

- I enjoy all sports and play football and volleyball regularly   4
- Play keyboard in a band with friends
- Member of University Physics Society and Film-Making Society

REFERENCES AVAILABLE ON REQUEST

Notes on the example hybrid CVs

William Lo Man Li

1. This CV uses a very focused and targeted profile to set out his experience and career aims. This profile doesn't need to mention William's skills as the 'Skills' section is immediately below.
2. The CV highlights skills relevant to sales.
3. Here, William notes a small number of the most relevant modules from his degree.
4. This experience is within a part of the motor industry: William notes the customer service aspects of the job, as these will be most relevant to sales, but also mentions wider responsibilities such as finance and operational management.
5. This role is highly sales-focused, including meeting targets, contacting customers and using product knowledge.
6. Retail is all about selling, so any retail experience is useful when applying for sales and marketing roles.
7. William's interests show his enthusiasm for cars and knowledge of this industry.

Adebayo Akinwande

1. Adebayo incorporates the skills he has gained from his degree into his 'Education' section. This is helpful when applying for jobs that relate directly to your degree, especially if you have little or no relevant experience outside your studies.
2. A survey of graduate recruiters[1] found that many consider that science and technology graduates are lacking in communication and teamworking skills, so it is particularly important for these graduates to highlight their skills in these areas and show where they have used them.
3. Attention to hygiene and quality are important in lab environments too!
4. This provides another chance to highlight teamworking and people skills.

Which style of CV will work best for me?

If you are:

- a student or new graduate with little experience outside education;
- applying for jobs which relate closely to the education and experience you have gained so far;
- applying for recruiters which tend to be traditional and conventional, such as law or accountancy firms

a chronological or hybrid CV is likely to work best for you.

If you are:

- applying for jobs which don't have any obvious link to your education and experience;
- trying to fit your CV closely to a job description/person specification;
- worried that gaps in your education and employment record may cause you to be looked on unfavourably;
- a mature student or career changer

a skills-based CV is likely to be a better option.

There are no set rules on which to use though – just use the style that you feel will set out what you have to offer as effectively as possible!

Finding out more

Prospects (2015) *Example CVs,* www.prospects.ac.uk/careers-advice/cvs-and-cover-letters/example-cvs Includes examples of traditional and skills-based CVs as well as academic, teaching and technical CVs.

TARGETjobs (2016) *Writing CVs for different kinds of graduate job,* https://targetjobs.co.uk/careers-advice/applications-and-cvs/270189-writing-cvs-for-different-types-of-graduate-job

References

1. Department for Business, Innovation and Skills Research paper no. 30 (2011) *STEM graduates in non-STEM jobs.*

What should your CV include?

What will you learn from this chapter?

Here you will learn what content you need to include in your CV: the different sections, why they are necessary and what you should include in each one.

You will also learn how to give your writing style impact, how to increase the effect of your CV via action words, which words and phrases are overused and so should not be included in your CV, and the importance of minimising jargon. The words you use in your CV can either give it a dynamic edge or make you come across as dull and uninteresting.

Heading and personal details

The first part of any CV is your personal details. You don't need 'Curriculum Vitae' as the heading. The less the selector has to read, the more he or she can focus on key facts; and if your CV is computer scanned, your name might just be recorded as 'Curriculum Vitae'!

Instead, start with your name in a large font size, say 18 points, so if the selector has a lot of CVs to view, he or she can quickly find yours. You don't have to give your full name; if your name is Christopher Robin Milne, it's fine to put 'Chris Milne'.

One graduate recruitment manager received a superb application but for some reason, the applicant had forgotten to add their contact details, so could not be contacted.

Next put your contact details: address, email address and phone number. Do include your email address as most recruiters will contact you via this. You don't need the words 'name', 'address', 'phone number' and 'email', as it's obvious what these are. Putting your address on one line (see below) can save space. Even your address isn't essential, as it's unlikely the employer will post anything to you, but the recruiter may want to know where you live, so you could just put the town where you live.

Robyn Hood

13 Lyndhurst Road, Sherwood, Nottingham. NT2 7SJ.
07777 764521   ab999@univ.ac.uk

In the United Kingdom, you don't need to include your age, date of birth, health, gender, race or marital status. The more personal details you supply, the greater the chance for discrimination. Some firms have instituted 'blind applying', where the selector is not given any personal details, to reduce discrimination.

Photos are not normally included in British CVs unless you are an actor, but in some European countries a photograph is standard (see Chapter 10: 'International CVs').

Should you include a profile or career aim?

Career Aims

A career aim or objective shows the employer you have a clear goal and gives a focus to your CV. It states the type of work you wish to enter. It can narrow opportunities if too specific, but something too general, such as, 'I wish to work in business', suggests you haven't done your research. Career aims should be short: no more than three lines long. They are easier to write than profiles and help prevent agencies submitting you for unsuitable vacancies. They can also help if you are changing career. If you have little work experience and a degree that is not relevant, a career aim can signal interest in a career. However, it is unnecessary when applying for a job in your degree subject area or if you have much relevant work experience.

Use a sensible email address, unlike the following

- demented.dinosaur@gnumail.com
- please_kiss_me@univ.ac.uk
- aardvark.mcdandruff@gnumail.com
- virgin_on_the_ridiculous@hotmail.com
- yourmywifenowjohn@univ.ac.uk
- sexylikewoaaaaah@univ.ac.uk

University researchers[1] created fictional CVs with both formal email addresses such as sannejong@hotmail.com and informal such as luv_u_sanne@hotmail.com. Recruiters rated applicants using a formal email address as more hireable than applicants using an informal address.

Underscores _ in email addresses were also disliked as they were obscured by the automatic underlining wordprocessors add to email addresses.

Exercise: write your career aim

Here are examples to get you started

- A computing graduate seeking a challenging software development role in a progressive technology company that rewards hard work and commitment.
- An English Literature graduate seeking an internship to gain practical experience and develop relevant skills in publishing.

Now write your own career aim here:

Profiles

A profile is an outline of your relevant skills and experience at the start of your CV, which allows selectors to quickly view key facts about you. It is a sales tool: a concise summary of your strengths. It's the CV equivalent of an interview suit in that it should create a strong positive first impression which entices the recruiter to read on. It differs from a covering letter, which explains in more detail why you are suitable for a specific vacancy and organisation.

Profiles are an introduction to your CV so should be at the start of your CV and not near the end, where some students place them.

Profiles can also be called **personal statements,** but we prefer 'profile': it's shorter. Don't call it **Personnel** Profile as students sometimes do: it's not just for HR! Profiles should be short – no more than six lines long, as they are appetisers to hook the recruiter into reading your CV. They can be either a paragraph or a bulleted list, but a paragraph is better at allowing your personality to shine through.

Profiles aren't essential. They work best for speculative applications or when a covering letter isn't needed, for example for CV databanks and for jobs where there is much competition for places, such as PR, advertising, consultancy and the media. They are less effective the more experience you have, so they work better for new graduates. Recruiters are cynical about profiles: a survey by Reed Recruitment found that 83 per cent of CVs included a profile, but that there was no correlation with success in getting interviews.

Don't include hackneyed phrases such as 'team player', 'good communication skills', 'hard worker', 'trustworthy', 'fast learner' and 'efficient', These send recruiters to sleep because they see them so often and, even worse, they are rarely backed up by evidence.

Exercise: which profile has more impact?

1. I am a dynamic and highly motivated graduate, and I have strong leadership and organisational skills.
2. Strong leadership skills demonstrated by captaincy of the university lacrosse team. Organised an event for the university RAG Society for 100 students, which raised £350 for charity.

The second profile is evidence based and so has credibility, whereas the first is just hot air. Back up claims made in your profile with evidence in the rest of your CV. If your profile says, 'strong leadership skills' but there is no evidence in your CV of your having taken leadership roles, the employer won't believe you.

Don't write your profile in the third person: 'David is seeking a post . . .' This sounds odd, as if somebody else wrote your CV for you. You can just avoid pronouns completely, as in the second example above: 'Strong leadership skills . . .', which makes your profile shorter. Do use full sentences and the word 'I' in your covering letter, however, as this gives warmth and a personal touch.

One retail bank advised, 'To say things like "I get on well with people" is meaningless unless backed up by example'.

Content of your profile

Say what you are doing now	Second year History student at the University of York . . .
Say what you're looking for	. . . seeking a summer internship in events management.
Match what they want • Core attributes and skills • Relevant achievements, experience, knowledge, training, qualifications or awards • What you enjoy doing: what motivates you	Publicity and events officer for the Asian Society, having successfully organised several large events. I take pride in all my work, thrive under pressure and love a challenge.

Exercise: now write your own profile

Write a profile for your CV in six lines or fewer. Follow the suggestions outlined above. Include a career aim and two or three strengths or achievements that are relevant to the job. Avoid writing about skills using such broad terms as 'communication' and 'teamwork', and using buzzwords!

Say what you are doing now.

Say what you're looking for.

Match what they want.

Education

Real quotes from student CVs
• I have a doable award in science
• I am doing a degree cause in orgasmic chemistry
• I am suspected to graduate early next year

The education section is more than just a list of qualifications: it can also show your ability to analyse information, solve problems, write effectively, plan and implement projects, and work without supervision. Normally, for a student or new graduate, education comes before work experience unless your work experience outshines your education but, once you've worked for a year or so, work experience will come first.

Education

BA (Hons) Business, Salford University, 2012–2015. Modules included:

Marketing 76%	Statistics 81%
Finance 58%	Law 59%
HR 67%	French 72%
Logistics 63%	Computing 66%

Final-year group assignment

Led a group of five students in planning and performing an experiment, analysing our results using SPSS software and making a presentation of complex information in a clear and concise manner, which gave me valuable experience in presentation skills and in time management. I learnt to communicate ideas and difficult concepts effectively, to write a report and achieve tight deadlines and achieved 81% for this project.

Canterbury High School, Canterbury 2005–2012

A Levels: Physics A, Chemistry C, Mathematics C

GCSEs: Eight, including Maths and English at grades A to C

You can summarise school qualifications as shown above, but mention important subjects, such as English and maths; you could list all of your grades if they are excellent. Put the highest grades first.

If your degree subject is relevant to the jobs you are applying for, then list relevant modules and grades: the more relevant your degree for the job, the more detail you should supply. A business student applying for finance might list many modules, but a history student applying for a similar role would simply give his or her degree title.

If you include a lot of modules, putting these into columns, as in the above example, looks smart and well organised, and makes the CV easier to read. However, it could confuse computer scanning software if it is sent to a large company or recruitment agency which uses this.

Projects or dissertations can give evidence for skills such as the ability to work independently, manage time, solve problems, give presentations and write reports. Group projects may be the closest thing to real work in your degree, so mention the role you took and how you coped with problems such as a lazy group member. Also mention any relevant technical skills gained during your course.

Employment

Real quotes from student CVs

- Over summer I worked for an examinations bored.
- Bartender for privet parties.
- As indicted, I have over five years analysing investments.
- Reason for living: Relocation.
- I am experienced in teaching marital arts including karate.
- I was responsible for terminating employees.
- I am a genital person. [instead of 'gentle'!]

This section can also be called Career History. Work Experience is appropriate if you haven't had much paid work, but Employment is nice and simple.

You can attract the selector's attention to the most relevant experience by grouping entries for this category under appropriate headings. Work experience can be divided into **Relevant Experience** and **Other Experience** headings, allowing you to put relevant work experience before other experience on your CV, even if it's less recent. You could also use other headings such as Computing Experience and Legal Experience.

RELEVANT EXPERIENCE

Bull and Morebull Solicitors, Leeds, July 2014
Three-week placement with a partner in the property department of a general practice solicitors' firm. Carried out research into a boundary dispute, attended Court and observed interviews with clients.

OTHER EXPERIENCE

Part-time Barman, The Drunken Sailor, Leeds, Sept. to Dec. 2015
Worked under high pressure, especially near closing time, and learned to deal tactfully with inebriated clients.

> One student wrote 'Relevant Experience'
>
> followed by
>
> 'Irrelevant Experience'!

Selectors want to see specific examples of relevant skills. Even working in a bar or restaurant can give evidence of ability to get on with people, to work under pressure and to work effectively in a team.

Write about skills you've gained in your work, such as the following:

- Teamwork
- Providing good customer service, for example showing tact when dealing with an angry customer
- Using humour to defuse a tense situation
- Selling, persuading or negotiating
- Exhibiting leadership
- Training, coaching, mentoring, motivating and giving feedback
- Using technical skills: computer skills such as spreadsheets, payroll or accounts systems and statistical, scientific and engineering techniques used in your work.

How often did you use these skills, and for what?

If your maths qualifications are weak, mention jobs you had that used maths or, for example, a successful statistics module. Most graduate jobs don't require trigonometry or algebra – just quick, accurate business maths: percentages and graphs.

Summarise addresses to keep things simple, for example

Burger King, Lincoln

Not

Burger King, 21 High Street, Lincoln, LN1 2SR

Try to keep all the details on one line. If the type of business isn't clear, say briefly what it does (accountants, international law firm, consultancy, etc.).

Don't criticise previous employers, or you could be perceived as a bad influence.

If you've done several similar routine jobs, it might be better to put these all together and then to state the skills you have gained afterwards. For example:

> **Part-time Waiter at Cafe Des Amis, Carluccio's, and Pizza Express during my degree (2013–2016)**
> In all of these jobs, I had to work in a busy team, sometimes under extreme pressure, and be positive and friendly with customers whilst providing a high-quality dining experience.

Volunteering experience may sometimes be more varied and substantial than that gained in paid work. It can come under 'Work' if you haven't had much paid work, or otherwise in the 'Interests' section.

Skills

The 'Skills' section normally comes after 'Employment', but if you have a skills-based CV, then this section may come earlier and be in more depth (see Chapter 5: 'Types of CV'). The skills typically included are computing, foreign languages and driving, but you can also give evidence for 'soft skills' such as leadership, teamwork and adaptability. The most important and relevant skills should come first, and you must give evidence of where you have used each skill. This section often works well in bullet-point format, with the name of the skill in bold at the start of the bullet, as shown below.

- **Spoken Communication.** Member of the editorial team for the University newspaper, which coordinated the sale of advertising space to local businesses.
  Sales adviser at B&Q: demonstrated knowledge of the different types of items sold and their uses, and responded effectively to customer queries.
- **Leadership.** As a student ambassador, I gave talks about university life to sixth form students, showed parents and potential students round accommodation and organised seating on buses between campuses.
- **Computer skills.** High degree of computer literacy with excellent skills using Microsoft Office, particularly Excel and Access.
- **Languages.** Good level of spoken French, basic Spanish.
- **Full, current, clean driving licence.**

If you speak any other **languages,** mention these, especially if you are applying for jobs which require language skills, and state the level to which you speak the language. A **driving licence** is essential for some jobs, such as sales executive, and useful in others. A good format is: 'full, current, clean driving licence'. In the United Kingdom, use the British spelling of 'licence' with a 'c', and not the US spelling, 'license'.

Computing skills are vital for many graduate jobs. MS Excel is one of the most common skills asked for by graduate employers, so if you are good at Excel, do mention this. Good knowledge of MS Office is sufficient for most jobs ('*Good working knowledge of MS Word and PowerPoint*'), but for a computing job, divide your skills into sections, for example:

- **Programming languages:** Java (three years' experience), C# (proficient), PHP (working knowledge), Python (basic knowledge)
- **Operating systems:** MS Windows 10, Linux
- **Applications:** Dreamweaver, Photoshop

Don't include outdated skills. One candidate who was struggling to get a job had included in their IT skills section 'Windows 95' which is the IT equivalent of saying you can ride a horse.

If you send your CV to a **CV bank** with thousands of CVs, selectors will find CVs by typing in key words, so mention relevant skills by name. See 'Applicant Tracking Systems' later in this chapter for more about this.

One student headed this section 'Working Kills' instead of 'Working Skills'!

Achievements

You don't necessarily need a separate achievements heading but it can suggest you can get things done.

The best way to write about your achievements is via a bulleted list. Items on the list should be short and to the point. Be concise, but make it clear what the achievement is: you can go into greater depth at interview. Put the strongest and most relevant ones first rather than using date order as dates aren't essential here. Go for quality rather than quantity: if you have more than six achievements, divide them into sections such as 'Academic', 'Sporting' and 'Awards', as long lists may not be read.

My greatest achievement was climbing to the highest point in the Netherlands

- **Designed and developed** a website for the caving club, with 400 page views each month.
- **Elected** 1st XI university hockey captain and led team on tour to the Netherlands, where we won every match.

If you have few examples of your achievements, you could combine this section with examples of leadership. If you can't think of any achievements at all, leave this section out and focus instead on relevant skills and strengths.

See Chapter 3: 'Analysing Yourself' for more help in identifying and writing about your achievements.

Interests

Real quotes from student CVs

- Extra Circular Activities' (should be 'Extracurricular': this mistake is very common).
- 'My hobbits include' – instead of 'hobbies'
- 'I played in a football team but I was not aloud to be captain.'
- 'In my spare time, I enjoy hiding my horse.'

One recruiter said that he read CVs starting from the end, as students' interests and voluntary work gave the best insight into their personality and how they were likely to fit the company culture.

It's better to show evidence of depth of involvement and serious commitment for a few interests rather than listing many superficial activities, or you may appear a 'butterfly' – someone who flits between activities without commitment. Long-term commitment to one activity suggests determination and dedication. Do, however, show a range of interests to avoid coming across as narrow: if all your interests are sporting, an employer may wonder if you could chat with a client with no interest in sport. Bullets can be used to separate interests into different types such as sporting, creative and artistic.

A recruiter for an environmental consultancy looked at the 'Interests' section of the CV first. If there wasn't evidence of outdoor interests such as sports or mountaineering, the candidate was likely to be rejected as they might not be comfortable in an outdoor role.

Don't make lists: 'Reading, cinema, sport' doesn't say anything useful, so give details of the level and frequency to which they are pursued and societies or achievements related to them.

Don't use clichés

Reed Recruitment[2] surveyed over 300 UK employers on what they looked for when reading CVs and found that one third of the recruiters said their biggest pet-hate phrase was '*I enjoy socialising with friends*', followed by 28 per cent who identified '*Good team player/ good working in a team or as an individual*'.

Competitive sports suggest you can work in a team and handle pressure, whereas playing a musical instrument to a high level shows commitment and perseverance, and if you have regularly performed in front of audiences, it suggests you won't be fazed if you have to give a presentation. Similarly, acting in a play requires teamwork, working to deadlines and the ability to cope with pressure.

Examples of how to write about your interests

- As captain of the cricket team, I set a positive example, motivating and coaching players and thinking on my feet when making bowling and field position changes, often in tense situations.
- As a volunteer youth worker in Birmingham, I needed energy and imagination to deliver results. I prepared young people for youth parliament, helping to equip them with skills required to take up their role in society; this included organising a visit to Parliament.
- As part of my church choir, I organised a gospel singing night for the university Catholic Society. I planned the food, performances, venue and publicity. Ninety students attended, and we raised £230 for charity.

Mention any interests that are relevant to the job. For example, an anthropology student wanting to get into investment banking would increase her chances if her application showed evidence of relevant interests such as a virtual portfolio of shares. Similarly, membership of the Society of Young Publishers would signal a strong interest in a career in publishing.

Mentioning only passive and solitary interests such as reading, Sudoku and watching films may suggest you lack people skills. If you do include these, then say what you read or watch. Evidence of leadership, taking responsibility and initiative are important for many jobs: captain or coach of a sports team, course representative, chair of a student society or scout leader.

Unusual interests add 'sparkle' to your CV and provide a talking point at interview: skydiving, for example, can show you like to challenge yourself and can withstand pressure. Unusual interests also help you to stick in the recruiter's mind: 'Oh yes, she's the candidate who teaches belly dancing.'

When you are still at school, your interests will play a major part on your CV, but will gradually diminish with time. Relevant interests will still count, for example if you are a school governor and are applying for a post in education.

'Hobbies and interests offer a window to your personality. All good CVs have one thing in common; they make the employer want to meet the applicant in person. How do they do that? For one thing, good CVs often include a hobby section that sends a strong message to a potential employer, confirming that the applicant is the right type of person for the job. Many applicants don't pay enough attention to the hobby section, and that apathy can work against you. Like other CV sections, your hobbies must support the all-important goal of getting the interview.'

—Advice from Whitehall Recruitment

References

Most companies will take up references before they hire you, and these are normally taken up after interview or once the employer has decided to offer you the job. You don't need to include your references on your CV unless a requirement to supply references has been stated. You don't even need to put, 'I'm happy to supply references on request.' If you are short of space leave this out; it's obvious you'll supply referees if you want the job.

The referee should know you well enough to be able to write positively about you and should know you relatively recently; a teacher you last saw years ago won't be able to write about your recent activities.

You wouldn't get references like the following now because of legal constraints:

- 'Not so much of a has-been, but more of a definitely won't be'
- 'Sets low personal standards and then consistently fails to achieve them'
- 'Would be out of his depth in a puddle'
- 'This student impressed by her determination to do as little as possible'
- 'Of all the people I have met, she was certainly one of them'
- 'Should go far and the sooner he starts, the better'
- 'Has reached rock bottom and has started to dig down'

And how not to ask for a reference:

- 'Will you please be a referee for a job for which I am appalling?'

Normally, employers ask for one academic and one employment reference. The academic referee may be your tutor, but if a project supervisor or seminar leader knows you better, you can ask that person to be your referee instead.

Your employment referee is typically an employer from a recent job. If you lack a suitable employment reference, then you can use a character reference instead, for example a family friend, teacher or sports coach.

Ask your referees' permission, and tell them about the jobs you're applying for. Sending them your CV and, if possible, the job description as well will allow them to write a more informed reference. It's important to keep referees informed about your progress, and when you get a job offer, do thank them for their help.

Some international applicants include **testimonials** with their application. These are open references given to the applicant by the referee to be used in any application, but are not greatly valued in the United Kingdom. There is no harm in including these, but the employer will still probably ask you for normal references.

How to write references on your CV

Include email addresses for your referees. Don't just give a phone number, unless your referee has said he or she prefers to be contacted by phone. Say what the referee's role is, or the recruiter may not know if your referee is a director or a cleaner!

Dr Wendy Woodhouse, Lecturer,	Debbie Hackett, Store Manager,
Business School	ASDA,
Durham University	Old Potts Way
Durham, DH1 3LE	Shrewsbury, SY3 7ET
ww999@durham.ac.uk	dh21@asda.co.uk

Example reference form

This is the type of form an employer might use to ask for a reference. These forms vary greatly, but it will give you some idea of the criteria you might be judged on.

Please rate the applicant on the following criteria:

	Strong	Average	Weak	
Makes decisions on own initiative. Willing to do what is required to get the task done.	Taking responsibility			Unable to carry out work without constant supervision. Reluctant to make decisions.
Plans ahead and breaks down objectives into manageable tasks with clear goals.	Organising			Struggles to plan ahead or to amend plans in response to changing priorities.
Can handle several tasks at once. Able to think and act quickly. Works well to deadlines.	Working under pressure			Doesn't work well to deadlines. Struggles with simultaneous tasks.
Shows determination to continue even when things are going wrong.	Facing challenges			Little resilience when facing obstacles. Easily loses focus.
Deals confidently with people. Influences via reasoned arguments.	Persuading			Lacks tact. Struggles to influence others via logic. Poor negotiating skills.

Please comment on anything else we should consider
(e.g. academic performance, integrity, personality).

How long have you known the applicant and in what capacity?

Action words

Certain active words in your CV and covering letter **can give these additional impact** and make a stronger impression. Instead of writing 'my work involved serving customers', you could instead write 'advising and helping customers and recommending products', which makes more impact.

Which of the following paragraphs makes the better impression?

1. *For my final-year project, I* **had to** *carry out a survey of patients' attitudes to health care services for the elderly. This* **involved** *interviewing patients in hospital and in their homes. A database* **was used** *to keep track of data collected. This project was* **finished** *on time and was awarded a 2.1 grade.*

2. **Devised** *and* **prepared** *a survey of patients' attitudes to health care services for the elderly as my final-year project.* **Interviewed** *70 elderly patients and* **obtained** *a substantial amount of data.* **Created** *a database to* **analyse** *and* **interpret** *this material.* **Completed** *this project three weeks ahead of schedule and* **achieved** *a 2.1 grade.*

The first paragraph contains a number of weak, **passive** verbs (in bold) whereas the second contains strong, **active** verbs (again in bold) such as devised and created suggesting a person who has initiative and takes action. The second paragraph also has the personal pronouns removed ('Devised' instead of 'I devised') which saves space and gives greater impact.

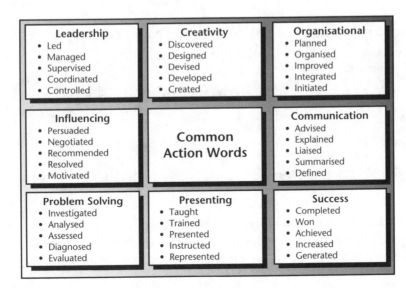

Leadership	Creativity	Organisational
• Led	• Discovered	• Planned
• Managed	• Designed	• Organised
• Supervised	• Devised	• Improved
• Coordinated	• Developed	• Integrated
• Controlled	• Created	• Initiated
Influencing		**Communication**
• Persuaded	**Common**	• Advised
• Negotiated	**Action Words**	• Explained
• Recommended		• Liaised
• Resolved		• Summarised
• Motivated		• Defined
Problem Solving	**Presenting**	**Success**
• Investigated	• Taught	• Completed
• Analysed	• Trained	• Won
• Assessed	• Presented	• Achieved
• Diagnosed	• Instructed	• Increased
• Evaluated	• Represented	• Generated

Exercise:

Try writing your work or interests sections of your CV, or your covering letter, using action words.

Admissions advisers at the University of Hertfordshire drew up a list of words which make a good impression in applications. These included *achievement, developed, planning, active, impact* and *involved*. Words which made a poor impression included *always, awful, bad, fault, hate, mistake, never, nothing* and *problems*.

Applicant tracking systems

Some large companies use computerised applicant tracking systems (ATS) that analyse candidates' fit for the job by scanning submitted CVs for keywords. Systems such as EmployAStar use artificial intelligence to parse the CV text and extract important information such as employment, education and skills, which then populates a CV database. Keyword searches rank CVs in order of suitability for particular vacancies. If your CV contains the keywords the employer wants, you will be ranked higher in the search results. Recruiters may only view the CVs of highly ranked applicants.

Simplified Applicant Tracking Screen

List name C# Developers in Birmingham area 14.27 07.11.16
Keywords 'C#', 'Developer'

Name	Updated	Rating	Status	Email
Rini Patel	04.10.16	*****	Contacted	rp312@mail.com
Dave Collins	19.09.16	*****	Contacted	dc12@gmail.com
Janet Lim	23.10.16	****	No contact	j_lim@yahoo.com

Keywords are words and phrases that describe attributes of the person required. The software is programmed to pick these words out so the words used on traditional CVs are less important. For example, in the statement

'I design websites using HTML and JavaScript' employers would search on HTML and JavaScript rather than design.

Some candidates have tried hiding lots of keywords in 'invisible' white text to try to get their CV to the top rank, but this is of doubtful effectiveness!

Making your CV scannable

Applicant tracking systems typically accept MS Word documents, PDF, .rtf, .html and .txt files. Other formats may not be opened and therefore not viewed.

Write your CV so that it includes keywords from the job specification. Most candidates send their standard CV without any customisation, which increases the chance of rejection because it doesn't include the required keywords to qualify for review by a recruiter. Very few companies now scan paper CVs.

Describe your experiences with concrete words: 'Managed the team' rather than 'Responsible for running the team'.

How to format your CV for scanning

- Use standard fonts in 10 to 14 points size. Fancy fonts may not survive the scanning process.
- Use bold or capitals for headings.
- Avoid graphics, boxes, shading and underlining.
- Avoid multiple columns as text might be interleaved from different columns making it unreadable.

Overused words and phrases

Certain words such as **dynamic** and **motivated** are so commonly used in CVs and covering letters that, instead of coming across as dynamic and motivated, you are perceived as lacking in originality.

These words are called buzzwords. The problem with such words is that they are rarely backed up by evidence. Below are some of the most overused buzzwords used in LinkedIn profiles.[3]

Avoid jargon

The company O2 in a survey of recruiters for its 'Think Big' programme found that using too much jargon can make candidates up to 72 per cent less likely to get the job. The following ten phrases were the most overused.

• Able to take a helicopter view	• Road-mapping
• Shifting the paradigm	• Strong interpersonal skills
• Blue sky thinking	• Leveraging my skills
• Out-of-the-box thinking	• Critical thinker
• Results-orientated	• Dynamic team player

It's normally better to use a simple word which has the same meaning such as 'using' instead of 'leveraging'. Don't use a complex word where a short, simple one will do.

CVs may be read by HR staff who may not understand technical terms, before being passed to the recruiting manager, so avoid unnecessary jargon. Also avoid using initials unless their meaning is well known (such as BBC) spell out the full words if they are unfamiliar.

Professor Daniel M. Oppenheimer[4] led studies on how language used can make you appear more or less intelligent. Researchers replaced shorter words in essays with longer words. Participants judged authors who used shorter words such as 'use' instead of 'utilise' as more capable and intelligent. The ease of processing information is strongly associated with positive qualities, including likeability, confidence, intelligence, and capability. Some graduates think that using long, complex words in applications will make them appear more intelligent but the opposite is true. If your writing is clear and simple, you will be viewed more positively.

Spelling and grammar

Spellcheck and then proofread your CV and covering letter and then give it to a friend to check again. Spellcheckers won't pick up 'form' instead of 'from' or 'sex' instead of 'six'! Grammatical mistakes are at least understandable, but spelling mistakes suggest you can't even be bothered to spellcheck your application.

If someone can't spell, they do not have the attention to detail we require in solicitors.

—Advice from a law firm

Exercise: spelling test

The following text contains at least 50 mistakes which have been found in CVs and covering letters. See how many you can spot. Although this is a humorous example, many of these mistakes do regularly crop up in applications!

Dear Sir or Madman,

I am sicking and entry-level position in pubic relations. I am suspected to graduate from my cause in orgasmic chemistry early next year and would like a salary commiserate with my experience. I would be happy to work in any part of England or Whales.

I am a conscious individual with grate writen comunication skills. I have a talent for working with commuters and I'm an acurate and rabid typist. I have lurnt MS Word computor and spreadsheet pogroms. I am also a prefectionist and rarely if if ever forget details. I have a proven ability to track down and correct erors and excellent memory skills, good analytical skills and excellent memory skills. I have an abilty to meet deadlines while maintaining my composer and can communicate information in an interesting manor.

When I worked in retail for a stationary company my responsibility's included oversight of are department, money-laundering duty's, sock control, customer liason and severing customers. It gave me an incite into business I received a plague for salesman of the year. I was also an administrator in a busty office, had an annual fudget and was instrumental in ruining the entire operation. My reason for leaving their was maturity leave.

As indicted in my Curculum Vitea my extra circular activities at university include vox pox for student radio, for two conservative years which enhanced my verbal comunication skils. My hobbits include marital arts and hiding my horse. I also own and maintain a volts wagon beatle. Formally, at secondary school I was a prefix and pier mentor.

I hope I have peaked your interest and expect to here from you shorty.

Miss S. Pelling

Here is the corrected version

Dear Sir or **Madam**,

I am **seeking an** entry-level position in **public** relations. I am **expecting** to graduate from my **course** in **organic** chemistry early next year and would like a salary **commensurate** with my experience. I would be happy to work in any part of England or **Wales**.

I am a **conscientious** individual with **great written communication** skills. I have a talent for working with **computers** and I'm an **accurate** and **rapid** typist. I have **learnt** MS Word **computer** and spread sheet **programs**. I am also a **perfectionist** and rarely **if** ever forget details. I have a proven ability to track down and correct **errors, good analytical skills and an excellent memory**. I have an **ability** to meet deadlines while maintaining my **composure** and can communicate information in an interesting **manner**.

When I worked in retail for a **stationery** company my **responsibilities** included oversight of **our** department, **money-lending duties, stock** control, customer **liaison** and **serving** customers. It gave me an **insight** into business and I received a **plaque** for **salesperson** of the year. I was also an administrator in a **busy** office; I had an annual **budget** and was instrumental in **running** the entire operation. My reason for leaving **there** was **maternity** leave.

As **indicated** in my **Curriculum Vitae** my extra-**curricular** activities at university include **vox pop** for student radio, for two **consecutive** years, which enhanced my verbal **communication** skills. My **hobbies** include **martial** arts and **riding** my horse. I also own and maintain a **Volkswagen Beetle. Formerly**, at secondary school I was a **prefect** and **peer mentor**.

I hope I have **piqued** your interest and expect to **hear** from you **shortly**.

Miss S. Pelling

Well done if you found over 50!

Quiz to test what you have learned

1. What is the best heading for a CV?
   A) Curriculum Vitae   B) Your first name and surname
   C) Your full name   D) CV for [your name]

2. UK Employers have no need to know your age, sex or marital status.
   A) TRUE   B) FALSE   C) PERHAPS

3. Your CV should include a personal profile or career aim.
   A) TRUE   B) FALSE   C) PERHAPS

4. You should not include any grades on your CV until you have actually obtained that qualification.
   A) TRUE   B) FALSE   C) PERHAPS

5. You should only include education from about age 11 and above in the 'Education' section.
   A) TRUE   B) FALSE   C) PERHAPS

6. You should give the complete name, address and postcode of your school, university and employers.
   A) TRUE   B) FALSE   C) PERHAPS

7. You should always include a section on hobbies and interests in your CV.
   A) TRUE   B) FALSE   C) PERHAPS

8. You should always give your tutor as a referee.
   A) TRUE   B) FALSE   C) PERHAPS

Answers are at the end of the chapter

Finding out more

References

1. Van Toorenburg, M., Oostrom J. and Pollet T. (2015) 'What a Difference Your E-Mail Makes: Effects of Informal E-Mail Addresses in Online Résumé Screening', *Cyberpsychology, Behavior and Social Networking*, 18(3), 135–40. doi:10.1089/cyber.2014.0542.

2. Cheary, M. (2016) *What Recruiters Are Really Looking for in Your CV*, www.reed.co.uk/career-advice/what-recruiters-are-really-looking-for-in-your-cv.

3. Sharma, M. (2010) *Most Overused Buzzwords Used in LinkedIn Profiles*, http://blog.linkedin.com/2010/12/14/2010-top10-profile-buzzwords.

4. Oppenheimer, D. M. (2005), Consequences of erudite vernacular utilised irrespective of necessity: problems with using long words needlessly. *Applied Cognitive Psychology*, 20, 139–156. doi: 10.1002/acp.1178

Further reading

1. Harrison, M., Jakeman V. and Patterson K. (2016) *Improve Your Grammar* (Basingstoke and New York: Palgrave).

2. Peck, J. and M. Coyle (2012) *The Student's Guide to Writing: Spelling, Punctuation & Grammar* (Basingstoke and New York: Palgrave).

3. Truss, L. (2003) *Eats Shoots and Leaves: The Zero Tolerance Approach to Punctuation* (London, Fourth Estate).

Quiz answers

1. **b.** Your first name and surname

2. TRUE. Although the first two can normally be guessed at!

3. PERHAPS. This can be useful but needs to be informative, factual and focused on the job in question.

4. FALSE. You can list any grades you have obtained until the present. It is often helpful to note your predicted degree class, and your grades will provide evidence to support this prediction (i.e. Upper Second [expected]).

5. TRUE. Education up to age 11 is not normally expected on a CV.

6. FALSE. This overloads recruiters with unnecessary information. Only include full addresses and contact details for yourself and your referees, and summarise other addresses.

7. FALSE. It is not the hobbies themselves which are important, but the way you present all the relevant aspects of your achievement and experience. Do not get hung up on this.

8. TRUE. Students and new graduates are normally expected to give the name of a member of academic staff as a referee, but this doesn't have to be the person formally assigned to you as a tutor if you prefer to use another academic who knows you well, such as a project or dissertation supervisor.

Well done if you got seven or more correct!

Making your CV look good

What will you learn from this chapter?

You will learn how long your CV should be, whether to go for a one-page or two-page model and when a longer CV is appropriate. This chapter also shows you how to make your CV look attractive and easy to read by careful use of layout, fonts and formatting. Visual impact is important: if your CV looks unprofessional, it may be discarded at first glance.

How long should your CV be?

One-page CVs

If 50 people applied to a vacancy, and each CV took ten minutes to read, it would take the recruiter more than eight hours – a full working day – to read them all, assuming this person did no other work!

Research at the BI Business School[1] found that employers may spend as little as 45 seconds skimming a CV before branding it 'not of interest', 'maybe' or 'of interest'. In such a short time, one-page CVs hold an advantage. Employers who receive many applications, such as investment banks, management consultancies, media employers and law firms, may prefer a single-page CV as they have many CVs to review. Single-page CVs also work well for speculative applications, which need to be concise to persuade the employer to read them. A CV is an appetiser: you should leave something for the interview rather than giving the recruiter indigestion.

❝I would have written a shorter letter, but I didn't have the time. ❞
—Blaise Pascal, mathematician, physicist and philosopher (1623–1662)

Surprisingly, one-page CVs can be much harder to write than longer CVs as you must make every word count, but they do show that you can write concisely – an underrated and important skill. It also shows you appreciate that the recruiter is busy and doesn't have much time. Single-page CVs work well when they contain lots of single-line bullets. Everything should be focused on the job you are applying for; consider every word, and discard all those that don't add value.

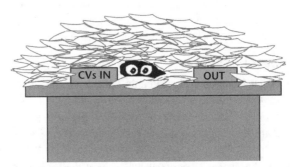

The Presenter's Paradox: quality over quantity

Studies[2] suggest that students believe that giving extra information in their CV will strengthen their case, but don't appreciate that selectors may adopt an 'averaging' approach, and the extra information may instead dilute their CV. Less can be more: you need sufficient information to impress, but not so much that the important information is diluted by irrelevancies.

Two-page CVs

Two-page CVs are the most common for British students. The most important information should go on page one, as some recruiters may only read the first page if they have many applicants.

Try not to leave a lot of white space at the end of your CV. A full one- or two-page CV suggests that you have more to tell the recruiter, but don't want to go onto an extra page, whereas a CV that finishes halfway down a page suggests that you've run out of things to say about yourself: you have nothing more to offer. A solution is to leave extra lines between sections, which improves readability, and to increase font size and margin width.

One-page casual work CV

James Joyce

47 Moon Road, Bath, BA38 8PQ 07766634669
email: jj@gmail.com

OBJECTIVE

I am seeking restaurant work over the summer in Bath and am available for work any time
from June to September. In previous jobs I have demonstrated organising skills, a sense of
responsibility and the ability to perform under pressure. I am able to relate to a wide range of
people, as proven by my varied work experience.

1

WORK EXPERIENCE

2

Waiter, Moneypenny Restaurants, Bath, July–Sept. 2014

Meeting and greeting customers, dealing with their enquiries, maintaining hygiene and
ordering stock. Also took phone bookings and orders. I learnt about working both on my
own and with others, and about working calmly under pressure, and greatly improved my
communication skills. I learned to use my initiative to handle stressful situations.

3

Client Assistant, Eastern Rail, Chelmsford, June–Sept. 2013

Developed my customer service skills so that the public felt at ease when asking for
assistance with their travel arrangements. Maintained a calm and positive demeanour, even
when dealing with angry passengers from delayed trains.

4

Other jobs have included housekeeping, and temping in a factory.

5

SKILLS
- **Providing excellent customer service** in customer-focused employment
- **Teamwork:** I enjoy working in both team environments and independently
- **Fast and proficient IT:** I am proficient with MS Word, Excel and PowerPoint.
- **Full, clean driving licence**

Interests and Achievements
- Captained the school hockey team that won the Essex Schools Cup.
- Organised many events at school, including a party for the elderly and a scheme for
providing help to first years for any difficulties they were facing.
- Assisted teachers by helping pupils with classwork and tutoring small groups.

6

EDUCATION

7

BA Honours English Literature 2:1, University of Bath, 2013–2016

8

Gold School, Chelmsford, Essex, 2006–2013
- 2013 A Levels: English Literature: B, Classics: B, Russian: B
- 2011 Ten GCSEs (A–C) including Mathematics, Double Science and French

9

This CV is targeted at summer restaurant work but, with small changes, could also be used for shop, pub or casual office work.

1. A clear, well-written objective can help you to stand out from the crowd. Avoid hackneyed phrases such as 'I have good communication skills and work well in a team'. Being prepared to work hard and to do almost any task are key attributes for casual jobs.
2. Normally, students put their degree before work, but for casual work during your course, evidence of relevant work experience and skills are of greater importance than the academic knowledge gained on your degree.
3. If this student were applying for a professional job, he would leave out routine tasks and duties, such as unloading, shelf restocking, cleaning and photocopying, but for casual jobs it's important to show your willingness to carry out mundane tasks.
4. If you can show you have useful skills and experience that can be put to good use from day one, you will be at an advantage over other applicants.
5. If you've done other routine jobs that aren't relevant, such as fruit picking or a factory assembly job, you could just summarise these as shown here. They provide more evidence that you are prepared to work hard and are adaptable.
6. Relevant interests and achievements give further evidence of people skills and taking responsibility.
7. Only brief details are given of academic qualifications, as they are not particularly relevant to the job.
8. French and mathematics GCSEs are mentioned. The latter shows numeracy, and the former may be helpful in serving the many tourists Bath gets.
9. No references are supplied at this stage. You only need to supply references when the organisation you are applying for asks you for them.

One-page investment banking CV

John Keynes

23 Danegate, York, YO1 3GA   07700900416   jk368@york.ac.uk   **1**

EDUCATION

BSc Economics   **University of York 2013–2016**   **2**

Predicted degree class: First, having achieved a First in Years 1 and 2

Including: Statistics 88%, Maths 91%, Financial Accounting 76%, Quantitative Economics 68%, Macroeconomics 71%, Financial Analysis 66%, Computing 75%

Cranley School,   **Bedford**   **2005–2012**   **3**

International Baccalaureate 2012 40/45 (top student in year).

Highers: Maths 6, Physics 6, French 7

GCSEs 2010: 10 GCSEs grades A–C, including English and French

EMPLOYMENT   **4**

Internship in Mergers and Acquisitions, HSBC, London June 2014–Sept. 2015   **5**
- Drafted due diligence summaries for private equity auctions
- Researched qualitative and qualitative information from a range of sources
- Delivered a presentation to clients on developing strategy to improve participation and engagement through technology
- Analysed financial and economic data for a report for future investment decisions

Team leader at residential camp, Brighton   **August 2014 (2 weeks)**
- **Responsibility:** looked after a group of nine secondary school children
- **Leadership:** motivated, inspired and acted as a role model
- **Assertiveness:** analysed situations to prevent problems in advance

Volunteer in Australia   **Sept. 2012–June 2013**   **6**
- **Communication:** fundraised by approaching people for donations
- **Adaptability:** worked in various teams. In the Cook Islands integrated different cultures by organising activities and games

SKILLS   **7**
- **Computing:** highly competent in Excel, Word and PowerPoint
- **Languages:** good spoken and written French, Japanese at JLPT N5 level

Interests and Achievements   **8**
- **President of University of York Investment Society:** ran a virtual portfolio that gained 25% in a year
- **International Maths Olympiad** 75% (class 1)
- **Travel:** have travelled on five continents and enjoy adapting to new cultures

---

This is a typical CV for investment banking. It packs a lot into one page and focuses more on achievements and responsibilities than on tasks and duties. Good presentation is important for all investment banking roles, but especially in areas such as Mergers and Acquisitions, where the work involves making a great many presentations.

1. **You don't need** the words 'address', 'phone number' and 'email address' as it's obvious what these are, and they just waste space.
2. **Education.** If you are still at university or left recently, your education should be at the top. If you don't give your academic results such as A-level grades, recruiters will assume they are poor. They will, however, be irrelevant once you have worked for a few years.
3. This student has done the **International Baccalaureate**, which is liked by many employers because of its focus on language skills and its rounded nature.
4. **Employment.** Say what the companies you worked for did, if this is not clear. Include locations. Mention products, departments – provide context. Think about challenges faced or any value you added.
5. **Include any achievements:** give numbers if you can ('portfolio that gained 25%'). Give dates and provide months as well as years if needed; for example, Dec. 2014–Jan. 2015 is very different from 2014–15.
6. Evidence of experience of other cultures can help for investment banking because of its cosmopolitan nature.
7. **Skills:** keep this simple – mainly languages and technical skills.
8. List several strong **achievements** which are quantified.

Two-page science placement CV

| Rosalind Franklin | 1 |

22 King's Road, London NW17 3YU   rf@gmail.com   0779005678   2

PROFILE

Second-year biology student keen to complete a laboratory-based internship this summer. Combined studies with work and other commitments, showing myself to be self-motivated and committed to achieving my goals. Demonstrated organising and problem-solving skills and capacity to take responsibility.   3

EDUCATION   4

BSc Biology predicted 2:1   University of Kent   2014–2017

Subjects included: 5

1st Year		2nd Year
Metabolism	63%	Pharmacology
Molecular Biology	67%	Physiology
Physiology	64%	Gene Expression
Chemistry	55%	Infection and Immunity

Practical skills gained during degree   6

Preparation and identification of nucleic acids, bacterial isolation and cultivation, immunoassays, spectroscopy, enzyme assays, protein purification, gene cloning, gas chromatography, HPLC, western blot analysis, and DNA and RNA extraction.

Research Project: 'The Effect of Molecular Chaperones on Yeast Prions'. Required that I work methodically and pay close attention to detail in order to achieve accurate results.   7

St. Paul's Girls' School, London   2007–2014   8

A Levels: Chemistry B, Biology A, Maths C

GCSEs: Eight, at grades A to C including maths and English

1. A **large font size for the name** makes it stand out and easier to find in a pile of CVs.
2. **Note how the address, email and telephone number are on one line.** You don't need the words 'address', 'email' and 'phone' as it is obvious what these are. Use a sensible email address.
3. A **profile or objective** can be useful, particularly if you are sending your CV to recruitment agencies where a letter may not be required. However, it isn't essential as this information can be included in a covering letter.
4. Subheadings such as 'Education' and 'Work Experience' can be larger than the body font to stand out.
5. The use of **tables to list modules** looks smart, suggests an organised person and makes the CV easier to read. You can add your module marks here if they are good. First-year modules are given with results, and second-year modules are just listed, as exams haven't yet been taken for these yet.
6. **Modules and practical skills help to sell your degree.** If you have a job description that lists technical skills you've used on your course, make sure these skills are mentioned in your CV, and research any you have not used. Employers may do keyword searches through CVs for specific skills such as HPLC or Excel. However, if you were going for a job that didn't involve lab skills, you could leave these out.
7. **Projects** are very important if you're looking for research work, as they are the nearest you will have come to doing real science work. You could sell the skills you had gained here:
   - Ability to work independently
   - Manage your time
   - Solve problems
   - Working in a team (for group projects)
8. **A Levels** on one line and summary of GCSEs to save space

WORK EXPERIENCE   9

Part-time Sales Staff   **Next, Croydon**   **Sept. 2012 – Feb. 2013**

Working in a busy store, dealing with customers giving high-quality customer care and ensuring sales targets were met. I was responsible for my own section and built strong, positive relationships with customers and staff.

Work Experience   **Guys Hospital, London**   **July 2011**

Shadowed a doctor in her clinics and helped patients.

10

Other jobs have included factory work and a paper round which involved getting up at 6 a.m. in rain or shine!

11

SKILLS

- **Problem-solving.** Continuous problem-solving exercises given as assessments, which required mathematical analysis and evaluation
- **Teamwork.** Have successfully undertaken various team projects within both academic and non-academic environments.
- **Communication.** Advised customers at Next, and responded effectively to customer queries. Developed knowledge of the different types of items sold and their uses. Delivered many presentations as part of assignments and projects on my course.   12
- **Computer skills.** Advanced user of Windows 10, MS Word, MS Excel and Access.

INTERESTS   13

- Organiser of RAG events, working in a team to plan and organise charity events, risk assess events, and liaise with venues.
- Peer mentoring: help new students settle into University life by meeting them in small groups to discuss any anxieties they may have.

14

REFEREES

Francis Crick,   Tina Watson,
Lecturer, School of Biosciences,   Manager,
University of Kent,   Next, High Street,
Canterbury, Kent, CT2 7NJ   Croydon, CR1 5RU
fc777@kent.ac.uk   tw@next.com
01227 764000   020 8777 5555

9. Although these are not science jobs, **transferable skills** are mentioned here. For example, people skills, teamworking skills, and communication skills are all valuable evidence that you could employ these in a science setting. Sometimes we see CVs from students with science and technical degrees which have no evidence of people skills at all: you wonder if, when they are sitting next to a friend, they text rather than talk with the person!

10. If you have done a lot of jobs, you can **summarise the more routine jobs** rather than filling your CV with lots of irrelevant information.

11. More evidence of relevant skills, focusing on some of the core competencies needed in science jobs. Notice how the skill is in bold at the start of the bullet to explain what it is about. This is a good place to use Action Words such as 'advised', 'developed' and 'delivered'.

12. **IT skills** are important: be specific about which programs you have used, rather than saying 'good IT skills'.

13. Show a range of interests, and focus more on social and active rather than solitary and passive interests. Serious commitment to at least one activity can be viewed favourably, as will evidence of getting on well with other people, for example in team sports. Independent or challenging holidays or foreign travel can also look good. Sell your transferable skills here: evidence of leadership, responsibility and communicating.

14. Normally you would give one academic referee (tutor or project supervisor) and one employment referee. Provide their job title and make sure you include their email address and phone number so they can be contacted quickly if needed.

CVs of more than two pages

Graduate CVs in the United Kingdom are normally no more than two pages in length but CVs for PhD graduates applying for postdoctoral research and lecturing posts can be much longer as they contain publications, conferences attended and teaching experience (see Chapter 9: 'Academic CVs').

CVs for highly experienced professionals can also be longer, but a new graduate should rarely require more than two pages.

A survey by CareerBuilder[3] found that 22 per cent of employers would reject candidates with CVs of more than two pages.

Keep related items together

There are certain design principles, called the Gestalt Principles of Grouping, which are relevant to CVs. One of these principles says that things that are close together belong together, so related information in your CV should be kept together. For example, education and qualifications are best grouped together under an 'Education' heading rather than under separate 'Education' and 'Qualifications' sections so the recruiter doesn't have to cross-refer.

Education

University of Birmingham, 2013–2016
Lincoln College 2011–2013
City School, Lincoln, 2006–2011

Qualifications

LLB Law: Upper Second Class
A Levels: Law B, Art B, History C
GCSEs: Nine, including English A and Mathematics B

Education

LLB Law, University of Birmingham, 2013–16
Lincoln College 2011-13
A Levels: Law B, Art B, History C

City School, Lincoln, 2006-11

GCSEs: Nine, including English A and Mathematics B

Boxes and lines make the CV look crowded

Don't centre all the text.

One employer received
a CV
in which the text was entirely centred
like this.
Her first thoughts were that she had
been sent a
restaurant menu.

However, another graduate got a job
in a top restaurant by designing her
CV to look like a menu!

Keep the formatting simple: if you have lines between sections, boxes, shading and tables your CV can look cramped. They also waste space, especially a rectangular box round the whole CV. Boxes may also confuse computer CV scanners. Tables with invisible borders can, however, allow modules or references to be neatly aligned in columns.

Blank lines make a better divider between sections, the white space giving a cleaner, more spacious look.

Alignment of text

The eye tends to scan down the left-hand side of the CV (unless the CV is in Hebrew or Arabic), so put headings and subheadings on the left rather than in the centre. Place the job title and employer before the date, as these are more important. In 'Education', put degree subject, then university and then date. Emboldening the job title/qualification and employer/college, as shown below, makes the content easier to read.

Waitress, Pizza Place, Croydon, July to Sept. 2015 Responsibilities involved . . .

BA Hons History (Upper Second), University of York, 2013–2016

Modules included . . .

Turn off justification of text (the justified text symbol is shown ringed to the right). Although justification gives a neat right edge to the CV, if you only

have   a   few   words   on   the   line,   it   can   lead
to   large   gaps   between   words,   as   shown   here.

Page margins

The standard MS Word setting of 2.54 cm for margins leaves room for the recruiter to write notes in the margins if the CV is printed but, if you are short of space, the 'Narrow Margins' setting in MS Word gives a 1.27 cm margin. This is the minimum you should use, as smaller margins risk text being cut off if printed or photocopied.

To save more space, use single line spacing (1.15 spacing looks smart).

Bold, *italic*, <u>underlining</u> and UPPERCASE

<u>Underlining</u> and UPPER CASE were used on typewriters for emphasis before the **bold** and *italic* styles became available. **Bold** and *italic* are much better for drawing the eye to key words and phrases, but use them sparingly.

Descenders and **ascenders** may be technical typographic terms but are important in affecting legibility. **Descenders** are the tails below letters. **Ascenders** are letters where part of the letter extends above the body.

<u>Underlining words</u> makes letters with descenders underneath harder to read, by cutting through the tails. Underlined words might also be misread if your CV is computer scanned.

UPPER CASE LETTERS lack the descenders and ascenders which increase legibility. This is why, in most countries, motorway signs no longer use just capital letters.

Which font should you use?

Don't use more than two fonts as this can look unprofessional. Stick to the conventional fonts suggested below, unless you are applying for graphic design jobs and wish to show off your knowledge of typography.

The choices for fonts are **serif** fonts, such as Times New Roman, which have curls on letters, called serifs, and **sans serif** (from the French 'without serifs') fonts, such as Arial, which lack tails.

Serif fonts

Some writers suggest you use Times New Roman or similar serif fonts for your CV. The 'Roman' fonts may not go back quite as far as ancient Rome (they originated in the fifteenth century) but they do look rather old-fashioned and might suggest that you are traditional in approach. Serifs alter the outline of letters, making them less legible for students with dyslexia or visual impairments. They also reproduce poorly on old monitors, which have lower resolutions than printed text.

Serif fonts have tails (circled).

Sans fonts don't.

Sans serif fonts

Most CVs are now initially read on screen and, as serif fonts don't read so well on screen, websites rarely use them. The BBC uses Arial and previously used Verdana, both sans fonts, as they are simpler, clearer and more modern in appearance. Google also use Arial. In the United Kingdom, two new sans typefaces were specially designed for use on road signs, as these must be quick to read.

Sans Fonts
This is Arial
This is Calibri
This is Verdana
This is Tahoma
This is Trebuchet
This is Lucida Sans
Serif Fonts
This is Times New Roman
This is Georgia

Fonts may be substituted when viewed on different computers, so choose a *'web safe'* font which looks the same on any system. These include:

- Serif fonts: Georgia, Palatino, Times New Roman
- Sans fonts: Arial, Helvetica, Lucida Sans Unicode, Tahoma, Geneva, Trebuchet, Verdana

One study[4] found Verdana to be the most preferred font as it reads quickly and is legible, and Times New Roman was least preferred. Another study[5] found that of 12 common fonts Tahoma was the quickest to read. Tahoma and Verdana were both designed for Microsoft for readability on screen and of the two, Tahoma has narrower letters and tighter spacing. Verdana is excellent if you have room for it, but Tahoma and Arial are more space efficient. If you prefer a serif font, try Georgia, which was designed for clarity on screen.

One font to avoid is Comic Sans: it looks a little childish and is inappropriate for CVs.

A student submitted his CV in 14-point Comic Sans font (like this). The recruiter said that it looked like it had been written by an eight-year-old.

Font size

The font size is expressed in 'points', referring to how big letters are.

18 points is a good size for your name at the start of the CV.

14 points works well for subheadings such as '**Education**' and '**Interests**' making it easy to pick out the main CV sections.

10 points is a good size for the normal body text of your CV in most fonts; it is big enough to read easily whilst conserving space. It is too small, though, in Times New Roman.

One study found that people using particular typefaces or smaller font sizes (within reason) were perceived as more intelligent: perhaps because a large font size reminds us of the way children write.

Colour

A classic dark colour, such as dark blue or burgundy (dark red) for your name and subheadings adds visual interest and makes subheadings quicker to distinguish. Dark colours also photocopy clearly.

The Gestalt Principle of Similarity says that the mind groups similar elements such as form, colour and size together, so CV subheadings such as 'Education' and 'Work' should be in the same font, font size, style and text colour, and bullets should be of the same size and shape.

> Only make very limited use of colour: one student had a CV with white text on a black background which, apart from looking strange, might use up all the black ink in the printer when printed.

Bullets or paragraphs?

Bullet points

Our brains love lists. They process lists more efficiently and retain the information with less effort. It's easier to extract the key points from small chunks of information as these are easier to read.

> Using bullet points on your CV can help you to write shorter, more concise and focused sentences that will grab the reader's attention. A concise CV is one that gets straight to the point; you don't want the person reading your CV to lose interest.
>
> —Advice from Whitehall Recruitment

Bulleted lists divide information into short, distinct items and appeal to our tendency to categorise. They hold our attention better and allow concise, dynamic sentences. Bullet points and CVs go together like bread and butter, allowing recruiters to quickly pick out relevant facts.

Use proper bullets such as round dots or squares. Bullets come in many styles, and unusual bullets might confuse scanning software.

- Circular or square bullets look more professional than
  - dashes or
  * asterisks.
- Proper bullets have the left hand text
  vertically aligned
  as shown here

– Incorrect bullets have a ragged
edge as
shown here

Long lists of bullets look boring, so limit the number of bullets in a list to about six. Try not to bullet every section of your CV, as having some sections bulleted and others in paragraphs adds visual interest.

Paragraphs

Paragraphs express complex thoughts and allow your personality to come through better than bullets. They allow more detail, nuance and depth of information, and demonstrate your writing skills better, but do take longer to read.

Keep paragraphs to a maximum of seven or eight lines as recruiters may skim over paragraphs longer than this. Instead, divide long paragraphs into several shorter paragraphs or use bullets. Don't let a paragraph or bulleted list spread over both pages of a two-page CV as this reduces readability.

Humanities students often use long paragraphs in their CVs, whereas students studying scientific and technical degrees tend to prefer bullets and short sentences!

Exercise: Hold your CV at arm's length

- ❏ Is it clear and easy to read?
- ❏ Does it have a pleasing, professional appearance, or does it look cramped, and overloaded with too much content?
- ❏ Are the main sections, such as 'Education' and 'Work', easy to pick out?
- ❏ For the job you are applying for, write down the key skills needed (see Chapter 4: 'Researching jobs and employers'). Then look at your CV for just 20 seconds to see if this information jumps out at you. If you can't pick it out quickly, then neither will the recruiter be able to.

How not to format a CV

Hilary Potter | 1

Tel. 01234 123456
12 Flagstone Terrace, Manchester, MM1 7RG | 2

Experience | 1

June–July 2015 Hayes Insurance, Office Assistant
Working   in   a   busy   office | 3

- clerical work, answering phones and entering information on database
- Liaising with other departments and arranging delivery of items

Jan.–May 2014 Waitress – Peggoty's Restaurant, York | 4
Took orders and served food and drinks to customers at tables in the dining room. Checked with customers make them feel welcome and comfortable and to ensure that they were enjoying their meals and took action to correct any problems. Gave out menus and took | 5
orders for food and drink. Prepared drinks and desserts, helped with washing up and cleaned tables. Took payments and gave change. Sometimes responsible for opening up and closing the facility.

YORKIST – UNIVERSITY MAGAZINE WRITER/CRITIC | 6
– Including cover article of summer issue with detailed | 7
research and work to deadlines

June 2015 Director of The Rocks: production for degree | 8
- Adapted for an outdoor performance

- Planned and led rehearsals | 9

- Edited the sound and bought costumes
=====================================
EDUCATION

2014 - 2017 University of York BA (Hons) History | 10
2010 - 2014   Bosworth High School, Manchester

| A Levels 9 GCSEs | History – A | English B | Maths – B | 11 |

1. Name and subheadings should be in larger font size to stand out.
2. Bold and italic are great for emphasis, but for a few words only.
3. Turn off justification of text to avoid strange text spacing.
4. Underlining can look old-fashioned and is less legible, especially under letters with descenders.
5. Avoid long, dense paragraphs with too much detail. Also the font and font size have changed here.
6. Upper-case words are less legible.
7. Use proper bullets rather than dashes, which don't wrap correctly here.
8. These are proper round bullets, but don't mix up bullet types in one CV.
9. Double-spaced lines waste space and look inconsistent here.
10. A blank line is needed between school and university, for clarity.
11. Boxes and lines make the CV look busy.

Finding out more

References

1. Arnulf, J., Tegner L. and Larssen Ø. (2010) 'Impression Making by Résumé Layout: Its Impact on the Probability of Being Shortlisted', *European Journal of Work and Organizational Psychology,* 19(2): 221–230.

2. Weaver, K., Garcia S. and Schwarz N. (2012) 'The Presenter's Paradox', *Journal of Consumer Research,* 39(3): 445–60.

3. CareerBuilder (2012) *Most Outrageous Resume Mistakes and Creative Techniques that Worked,* 11 July, www.careerbuilder.com/share/aboutus/pressreleasesdetail.aspx?sd=7/11/2012&id=pr707&ed=12/31/2012.

4. Bernard, M., Lida B., Riley S., Hackler T. and Janzen K. (2002) *A Comparison of Popular Online Fonts: Which Size and Type Is Best?* Software Usability Research Lab, Wichita State University, http://usabilitynews.org/a-comparison-of-popular-online-fonts-which-size-and-type-is-best.

5. Bernard, M., Mills M., Peterson M. and Storrer K. (2001) *A Comparison of Popular Online Fonts: Which Size and Type is Best?* Software Usability Research Lab, Wichita State University, 10 January, http://usabilitynews.org/a-comparison-of-popular-online-fonts-which-is-best-and-when.

Creative and Media CVs

Contents

What will you learn from this chapter?

We will look at what makes a creative CV and whether or not they are effective; view some example creative and media CVs; give tips on how to design one and finally see some examples of even more creative ways to sell yourself.

> A student stapled a teabag to his CV along with the message *'I enclose a teabag so you can enjoy a cuppa while perusing my CV.'*

What is a creative CV?

Creative CVs use unusual layouts and shapes, colour, graphics and even 3D in a bid to stand out and attract attention. They are often used by design and architecture students to showcase the design skills and creativity required in these jobs, but may be used for any jobs where there is a lot of competition, to help a candidate stand out.

Do creative CVs work?

In a study[1] by BI Business School, recruitment professionals were given the same CV content in three versions: formal, creative and on coloured paper. The formal CV was most liked by recruiters, and all divergences from the formal format reduced the chances of interview. Coloured paper had a negative effect, and the 'creative' format was the least liked: the same candidate had almost twice the chance of being offered an interview with a formal CV as with a 'creative' one.

For some jobs, such as graphic design and architecture, a creative CV can be effective, but it is the content and presentation that makes the impact, and not gimmicks: eccentric CVs can turn off employers. For jobs with high competition for places, such as those in the media, you may need to take more risks to get your CV noticed, but even here, content is king: the best looking CV will not get you interviews if the content is weak.

Don't let the medium impede the message

Get the content right before focusing on the design. The BBC once said that if you baked your CV in a cake and sent it to them, it would get eaten . . . and nothing else; they want everything in the same professional format. Students applying for design jobs are expected to present a smartly designed CV, but it must balance being eye-catching and unusual with showing a professional approach.

Designer CVs are high risk. Some employers may love your design, but others might hate it, so get other peoples' opinion before you send it out. One large advertising agency recommended a standard CV, but smaller agencies may be more captivated by an unusual CV, as they have fewer to read.

You could design your CV using professional publishing software such as InDesign, which allows sophisticated visual effects, but convert it to PDF format before submitting. If your CV includes lots of graphics leading to a large file size, it might be blocked by spam filters, so as well as attaching your CV, you may wish to include a link to your online CV in the body of your email.

If your CV is on paper it will have to be filed, and unusual sizes and formats such as 3D CVs can make this difficult. If it is on the label of a beer bottle in microscopic text (see below), or printed on a T-shirt, it will be hard to read as well as hard to file. Book-format CVs (folded into four A5-size pages) are difficult to copy and to read. Landscape format CVs (wider than they are long) are harder to design but can stand out from the crowd.

The beer CV

A graduate printed his CV on the packaging of his own home-brewed beer. He sent packs of the beer to marketing agencies, labelling each bottle with part of his portfolio and a link to his CV. He described the beer and himself as smooth and elegant, with a bit of a wild side, and got three job offers.

You can give your CV a distinctive brand identity by using the same theme, fonts and colours as your website and portfolio. Some students have even designed their CV using the colours, font and style of the logo of the company they are applying to. A subtle watermark or border can be effective. At the very least, your covering letter should use the same font as your CV.

What skills can you sell in your creative CV?

Creative CVs take a lot of work to get right, and if you are not careful, the layout may detract from the key purpose of the CV: showing how your skills relate to the job. Employers are most interested in the content, plus what you have created, such as listings of exhibitions. For a digital arts CV, include technical skills such as Maya and Photoshop. For advertising jobs, evidence of interest in music, art, photography or film may help.

Creative practitioners now need a wide skill set to make the most of digital media. Small creative businesses and freelancers can now publicise products as effectively as larger organisations via the Web. Here are some skills you could sell on a creative CV by giving examples of when you have used them:

- **Self-management:** much of the work in the creative industries is self-employed/freelance.

- **Ability to work in multidisciplinary teams:** if you are a web designer or animator, you may be working alongside programmers and sound engineers.
- **Versatility:** you show the ability to work in a range of formats.
- **Problem solving:** you are able to deal with the inevitable setbacks that occur.
- **Resilience:** you can manage instability and pressure and are persistent even when there are major obstacles to be overcome.
- **Multitasking:** you may be working on a number of projects with different clients at any one time.
- **Time management:** You can work quickly, to tight deadlines, with high quality!
- **Networking and social media:** you have skills in self-promotion and creating publicity.
- **Entrepreneurial skills:** you can promote and develop your business.
- **Negotiation:** you can negotiate contracts with clients.

Portfolios

Creative directors look at CVs to decide whether to bother looking at your portfolio: looking at a website takes time, and anyone who can't format their CV properly won't be of much use! Creativity is demonstrated by your portfolio rather than your CV, so let your work do the talking.

- Host your portfolio on a website for easy access and provide a link from your CV.
- Go for quality, not quantity: employers may only spend a few minutes looking at your portfolio, so pick your strongest work.
- Lay out your portfolio in a logical order.
- All items must be easy to understand: add a short description for each piece, saying how and why you produced it and describing any problems you had to overcome in its production. You could also include a short statement on your work and artistic influences.
- In the creative industries, Instagram feeds are partially replacing CVs and portfolios. Instagram portfolios may also include information on your

activities outside work. Directors now use Instagram to vet candidates as they can get a feel for your personality as well as your artistic skills.

A survey by the University of Lincoln found that 100 per cent of design employers surveyed expected candidates to showcase their design work at application by a mini-portfolio attached to the CV; 71 per cent on the CV itself; and 29 per cent via a web link. None of the employers wanted a DVD, or a CV with no design work included.

Example creative CV

William Morris

07891 855555　morris666@yahoo.com　**1**
Portfolio vimeo.com/wm Blog wordpress.com/wm
LinkedIn.com@morris311　**2**

BSc Multimedia Design, Exeter University, 2013–2016
- **Modules:** 3D Modelling, Visual Effects, Digital Photography
- **Project:** Created 3D animation of Nordic Saga. Extended skills in post-production with AfterEffects. Graded 78%.

Marlborough College, Wiltshire 2008–2013
BTEC Art and Design (Distinction)　**3**

At work

Rossetti Textiles, Oxford, Summer 2015　**4**
Developed web applications for clients, and administrative tools. Tested my ability to use my degree skills in the real world.

Telesales, Burne-Jones plc, Oxford, July–Sept. 2014
Greatly enhanced my telephone and persuasive skills

Clients

Created a new website for roofing company, www.kelmscott.com.

Awards

Prize for best final-year university project　**5**

Why me?

Ideas-driven: can visualise and quickly develop new concepts
Well organised: can tackle challenging and complex tasks　**6**
Self-starter: can meet tight deadlines in fast-paced settings

Skills

Alias Maya ✓✓✓✓✓
Dreamweaver ✓✓✓✓✓　**7**
AfterEffects ✓✓✓✓✓

Spare time

8

9

Although this CV is creative, it can still be easily read, photocopied and printed.

1. **Stylish font** for the name and subheadings: unusual fonts are acceptable for design roles, but they must still be easy to read.

2. You can use **more colour** in design CVs, but make sure that the CV is still legible if photocopied in black and white. Tastefulness is important in creative CVs: garish, inappropriate colours may get you rejected.

   Include a **link to your portfolio** and any other relevant material such as a blog or website you have designed.

   Icons for sections, such as the Mortar Board and Scroll here, instead of an 'Education' subheading can add visual interest.

3. For the BTEC Award some students write 'D' instead of 'Distinction'. This is unwise as employers who are unfamiliar with BTEC might assume that this is a low grade.

4. **Informal subheadings** can express individuality:
   'At work' instead of 'Work Experience'
   'Why me?' instead of 'Personal Statement'
   'Spare Time' instead of 'Interests'

5. **Awards and prizes** are important.

6. **A list of relevant skills** for design work rather than the hackneyed 'Good team worker' type of generic skill.

7. **Tick boxes** are a different way to indicate technical skill levels.

8. **A pie chart of interests** is an unusual way to present these but doesn't give much detail. Mention relevant interests, such as teaching photography, here.

9. **Two columns** – right-aligned in the left column and left-aligned in the right – creates an interesting appearance.

Example architecture CV

The following example is a CV for an architecture student. Down one side, images of the student's work are featured, but the CV must also include a link to the applicant's full portfolio. Include your CAD (computer-aided design) skills. The background of the CV is white so employers can print it without wasting lots of ink. Although this CV is for architecture, you could also use this CV style for design roles.

You could attach a mini-portfolio in PDF format with your CV, with a more comprehensive selection of samples of your work. Only have a few pages, and keep the file size below 5MB as larger emails might get blocked.

Frank Wright

2 Bridge Road, Leeds, L2 3AG 01223678993
flw36@leeds.ac.uk

Portfolio www.googlesites.com/flw

EDUCATION

BA (Hons) Architecture, University of Leeds 2013–16
Upper Second Class Honours
Modules included architecture practice, urban design and
building construction.

Derby School 2006–13
A Levels: Art A*, Graphics A, Maths C,
10 GCSE's grade A*to B, including graphics A*, Maths A

EXPERIENCE

Drew Murphy Architects, Leeds, Sept. 2014
Integrated work with my studies, obtained skills in Google
SketchUp and learned to work quickly to high-quality
standards.

Crystal Architects, Derby, July 2012
Focused on housing developments in Nottingham.
Produced visual perspectives from technical drawings
which enhanced my ability to translate 2D to 3D.

Sales Assistant, ASDA, Derby, Aug. 2012–May 2013
Part-time job: serving customers, working in a busy team
and ensuring cash procedures were carried out.

INTERESTS
- President of University of Leeds Photography Society.
- Leeds School of Architecture. Attended lectures by
  guest architects.

ACHIEVEMENTS
- Won the Leeds School of Architecture design competition.
- Advanced computer skills in 3D Studio MAX, AutoCAD and Photoshop.

Example media CV

Georges Méliès

OBJECTIVE: To begin a career in the media where my creativity, initiative and passion for the media would allow me to progress.   1

RELEVANT EXPERIENCE

Production Runner, Antiques Roadshow, June–July 2016   2
- BBC work experience: location and live filming: runner, soundman
- Research: current affairs, web, archive
- Working in a busy office: clerical work, answering phones

Director, 'Flash', University Film Club production. Jan.–May 2015   3
- Planned and led rehearsals; directed crew and actors on location
- Organised filming and script meetings; co-wrote script

EDUCATION

BA (Hons) English, Upper Second, University of Sussex, 2013–16   4

Hogwarts Academy, 2007–13
A Levels: English: A, Drama: B, French: B
9 GCSEs: 4 at A grade including Maths and English

SKILLS   5
- **Problem solving:** managing complex projects with budgetary and time constraints
- **Creativity:** writing film scripts; directing a play; co-directing a film
- **Fast and proficient IT:** Adobe Premier, HTML and JavaScript

INTERESTS   6
- **Television:** watching intelligent drama and writing reviews
- **Social media:** active Facebook, Twitter and LinkedIn accounts and write a blog
- **Cinema:** discussing film; reading critical works and blogging about films
- **Creative writing:** currently writing a short film screenplay

OTHER EMPLOYMENT   7
Assistant Administrator, LV= Insurance, June–Sept. 2015
Worked under extreme pressure in busy periods and developed sensitivity to clients' needs when dealing with claims.

Georges Méliès gm@hotmail.com   0774567882   8

Media CVs must be of high quality as the media is one of the most popular career areas. You may think it's a great idea to set out your CV as a mock-up of the front page of a newspaper, but employers will have seen these before. Similarly, bright colours will annoy rather than impress: content is what counts.

1. A well-written objective or profile can help you to stand out from the crowd in this competitive field.
2. Normally students put their degree before their work experience, but this candidate has got strong media work experience and felt that this was a stronger selling point than their non-media degree subject.
3. Enthusiasm for the media should be demonstrated in relevant student societies and voluntary work. This candidate has been involved in the Film Club, written reviews and gained relevant work experience.
4. Only brief details are given of academic qualifications, as they aren't that relevant to the media.
5. For media jobs, practical skills may be more important than your degree. There is no room for passengers in the media, so if you can show you have useful skills and experience that can be put to good use from day one, you will have an advantage. Skills you could emphasise include:
   - Tact to work sensitively with people who are under pressure
   - Stress tolerance in pressurised situations with tight deadlines
   - Energy to work extremely long hours when required
   - Flexibility and ability to multitask
   - Evidence of networking
   - Evidence of achievements and initiative
   - Evidence of problem solving
   - Relevant technical skills
6. Media employers often say that what makes a CV stand out is passion for the media. Your CV must convey this passion and the person behind it. Your enthusiasm, motivation and initiative should come through in the CV itself and the covering letter which gives you the opportunity to demonstrate not only these qualities but also your writing skills!
7. Non-relevant employment is near the end of the CV as it's less important but still provides evidence of relevant skills such as tact and ability to work under pressure.
8. Contact details are given in the footer at the end of the CV. This is unusual, but in one sense, logical: the employer shouldn't need to contact you until after reading your CV.

Being extra creative

One technique that might work for jobs involving presenting to clients is to make an animated CV using Prezi or Powtoons. Prezi (http://prezi.com) is presentation software similar to PowerPoint, but allowing you to zoom into and rotate content. Powtoons (www.powtoon.com) allows you to make cartoon-like animated video CVs.

Finally, here are some ways people and companies have been even more creative:

- One job hunter made her CV into the wrapper for a chocolate bar which proved popular with recruiters! On the back it listed 'Ingredients' which included motivation, analytical skills, innovation, versatility and creativity.
- A graduate had been trying without luck to get into investment banking. As a last resort, he printed 100 postcard-sized CVs and placed a CV on the windscreen of every luxury car he found in the financial heart of London. The next day, he got several calls offering him interviews from the managers who owned the cars. We don't advocate this approach as another graduate jobseeker put up 200 poster-sized CVs and was fined for bill posting.
- One Halloween the recruitment company InAutomotive found carved pumpkins on their doorstep each with a CV in the middle. The pumpkins had been carved to read 'GIVE ME A JOB!' The person who placed them there was later interviewed for a marketing job.
- A graphic design student created a Lego mini-figure of herself in business dress for an advertising CV, which highlighted her skills.
- A student turned his CV into a GQ magazine, gaining an internship at GQ without even being interviewed. The magazine contained stories about his life, education and work experience, and why he should be recruited, plus photos of the candidate, a contents page and an editor's letter.
- A jobless graduate handed her CV to fellow train passengers and was offered a job.
- A graduate made his CV into a computer game to show off his coding skills to employers. You can view it at http://ow.ly/qCmeM.
- IGN Entertainment launched a programme to teach programming to passionate computer gamers with little coding experience. Instead of asking for CVs, IGN posted challenges on its website such as estimating

how many pennies lined side by side would span the Golden Gate Bridge. It also asked candidates to submit a video CV showing their love of gaming. Six candidates were recruited, of whom several were non-traditional applicants with little college education or work experience, who would not have been selected on the basis of their traditional CVs.

The strange case of the scented letter

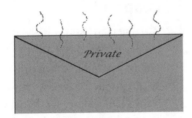

A student who had been rejected by the main advertising agencies bought some pink envelopes and a small bottle of expensive perfume in early February. He placed his CV in the envelopes and wrote 'Private' on the outside. He liberally sprinkled the envelopes with scent and posted them to the senior partner in several large agencies. When they arrived, nobody dared to open the letters and the graduate was offered several interviews: presumably for his daring. Note that we don't recommend this approach!

Finding out more

Useful websites

Creativepool (www.creativepool.co.uk) allows students to upload examples from their portfolios.

CV Parade (http://cvparade.com) is a great website to archive your creative CV or get ideas for it.

References

1. J. Arnulf, Tegner L. and Larssen Ø. (2010), 'Impression Making by Résumé Layout: Its Impact on the Probability of Being Shortlisted', *European Journal of Work and Organizational Psychology*, *19*(2): 221–30.

Academic CVs

Contents

What will you learn from this chapter?

You will learn about the differences between academic CVs and CVs for other jobs, and how to use an academic CV to apply for academic jobs or postgraduate study. This chapter also explains how to set out an academic CV, what to include in it and what not to include.

What is an academic CV?

The term 'academic CV' can refer to either of the following:

- A CV produced to apply for lecturing and research posts in higher education
- A CV produced to apply for a programme of postgraduate study or research

The former are normally much more detailed and specialised than the CVs that have been covered in earlier chapters and this chapter will focus on these. First, though, we will look at applications for further study at both master's and PhD level.

CVs to apply for taught master's degrees

These are generally similar in length to other CVs produced by new or recent graduates: not more than two pages (although if you are applying for a master's that requires previous professional experience, such as healthcare, then a slightly longer CV may be acceptable).

The most important things on applications for master's courses are your grades at undergraduate level, your academic reference and your personal statement. Again, professional experience may be important for certain courses or subject areas.

While you are often invited to attach a CV to your application, it is not likely to be as important as it would be for a job application. If the university you are applying to has asked you to send a transcript of your grades, your CV does not even need to go into any great detail about your current or most recent degree.

You may even be able to keep the CV to one page, focusing it on your studies, any relevant activities or work experience and involvement in university life outside your studies. You won't need to go into detail about any part-time jobs or general interests.

The personal statement should show your motivation for undertaking postgraduate study (including your reasons for applying to that particular university) and how your undergraduate degree, and any other experience, has prepared you for this. Your careers service or academic department will be able to provide help and advice on writing your personal statement.

References for postgraduate study

Employment references are less important when you are applying for postgraduate study, whether through research or taught master's courses. You could give more than one academic referee – perhaps a tutor and a project or dissertation supervisor. If you are asked to submit references online with your application, you don't need to include any mention of references on your CV.

Angelica Kaufmann

121 Darkness Way, Swansea SA2 1MA
Tel. 07700 900987 email angiekaufmann94@mail.com

EDUCATION AND QUALIFICATIONS

2011 – 2015   University of Leicester,

BA History of Art with a Year Abroad

- Achieved a high 2.1 (68%) with First Class results in two modules
- Completed a 10,000-word dissertation on 'Medievalism and Symbolism in the work of Sylvia Fein', which was awarded a grade of 80%   **1**
- Awarded the Faculty prize for the best dissertation of 2015
- Completed a year of study at the University of Montpellier, France

2004 – 2011   Shriftgrethor Technology School, Swansea

- A Levels: English (A), Fine Art (A), History (A), French (B)   **2**

RELEVANT EXPERIENCE   **3**

2015   Visitor Assistant, Purple Square Gallery, London E1

- Three-month voluntary part-time internship
- Assisted with exhibition planning and curatorial research
- Wrote press releases and catalogue entries
- Liaised with artists, dealers and visitors

2014   University of Leicester Fine Art Society   **4**

- Curated an exhibition of student artwork
- Gave a presentation at the launch of the exhibition
- Responsible for cataloguing the artworks

INTERESTS   **5**

- Fashion: set up the University Fashion Society and have designed and made clothes for myself and friends
- Painting and photography: have exhibited at the University art gallery
- Travel: Recently visited Mexico, where I was able to see many of the works of Frida Kahlo, Leonora Carrington and Remedios Varo.   **6**

SKILLS   **7**

- Good knowledge of French, Spanish and Italian
- Competent in all MS Office programmes
- Familiar with library cataloguing and specialist art databases

Notes on Angelica Kaufman's CV

This is an example of the type of brief CV that a final-year student or recent graduate might submit with their application for a taught master's course in a similar area to their bachelor's degree. Note the following points:

1. Include any academic awards or prizes.
2. You don't need to go back beyond your A Levels on an academic CV.
3. There is no need to include any work experience that doesn't relate to your postgraduate application.
4. Include extracurricular activities that relate to your degree: these show that you have a genuine passion for your subject.
5. Again, only include interests that link to your chosen course of study or that show your involvement in and contribution to University life.
6. If you include travel as an interest, say what you got out of it and how it relates to your studies: this is much more relevant than just listing the places you visited!
7. IT and language skills will be relevant for many areas of postgraduate study. You may also include specialised skills such as lab techniques, specialist IT packages and practical skills such as film-making and computer repair, if appropriate.

CVs to apply for PhDs and other research degrees

As with applications for taught master's courses, your personal statement will be more important than your CV. You will also be expected to submit a research proposal, outlining your intended area of study, why it is significant, how it fits with the work of the department and what you can bring to it.

The CV itself, as the following example shows, is similar to that for a master's degree, focusing on your academic record and any related experience or achievements. Include an outline of your master's dissertation or project and any further academic awards or prizes. If you have already begun to publish academic papers, or present your work at conferences, be sure to mention this in your CV.

Your research proposal needs to convince potential supervisors of your enthusiasm and demonstrate your knowledge of your subject area. It should cover issues such as the research questions or hypotheses you plan to work on, your proposed methodology and what you hope to achieve through this research. Writing a good research proposal is not easy and you should seek advice from academics, in particular people who have supervised your master's or undergraduate dissertations, as well as referring to print and online resources.

Rob Stephenson

1 Baxter's Place, Bridge of Don, Aberdeen AB2 8HR
robert.a.stephenson.22@aberdeen.ac.uk 07700 900464

EDUCATION

University of Aberdeen, MEng Civil Engineering, 2012–2017

- Courses included: Stress Analysis; Design of Structural Elements; Oceans and Society; Mechanics of Structures; Design of Structural Elements; Structural Dynamics; Environmental Engineering
- Fourth-Year Project: Concrete Carbonation in Marine and Littoral Environments

Bell Rock Academy, Angus, 2006–2012

- Advanced Highers: Mathematics (A); Physics (B)
- Highers: Mathematics (A); Physics (A); Chemistry (B); Computing (B); German (B)

RELEVANT EXPERIENCE

Summer Intern, Institute of Marine Engineering, Science and Technology (IMarEST), June–September 2015

- Analysed scientific literature relating to the development of lightweight materials for use in offshore wind turbine construction
- Consulted with energy and construction companies to gather further information on the construction and maintenance of wind turbines
- Produced a report for presentation at a conference

Student Ambassador, University of Aberdeen, 2014–2016

- Visited local schools to inform secondary students about their options for studying science and engineering at University
- Delivered presentations to encourage students to consider going into higher education
- Answered students' questions about both university life and engineering topics

SKILLS

Competent in AutoCAD, SolidWorks, Matlab and MS Office

PROFESSIONAL MEMBERSHIPS

Student member of the Institution of Civil Engineers (ICE) and the Institute of Marine Engineering, Science and Technology (IMarEST)

CVs to apply for lectureships and research posts

Academic CVs for these posts are a bit of a law unto themselves. They ignore the guidelines on length given earlier in this book and can run to several pages. Part of the reason for this is that they include a number of extra features that would have no place in a CV for other jobs, such as publications and research interests.

Competition for academic posts is fierce and you need to demonstrate more than just high academic achievements – these will be taken for granted. Universities look for people who can not only teach, research and publish but who can also manage the administration and other activities that go with the core academic work. One of the most important of these is writing bids for funding to support your research.

Don't just think of your academic CV as a long list of factual information. Like all CVs, it is a marketing document and needs to show the university how well you fit their requirements. It is important to tailor every application you make to fit that specific university and department. Analyse the job description and person specification to pick out the research interests and the key skills and experience required. Research the department and individual members of staff within it; think about how your research interests and teaching experience would fit in and what you could add to their work. You should also research the university more broadly: most university websites will carry details of the university's policies, strategies (including their research strategy) and annual reports, as well as news pages highlighting the university's successes. External sites, such as university league tables, will also be useful.

These CVs should be set out in reverse chronological format. Although academic CVs can be longer than other CVs, don't feel that you have to cover many pages, especially if you are just starting out on your academic career. Three or four pages are fine for new PhDs and early-career researchers.

Note that academic CVs should only be used for academic jobs – jobs in universities and other higher education or research institutions with titles such as 'Lecturer', 'Research Associate' or 'Teaching Fellow'. If you are applying for other university job roles, such as administration and support jobs, you should use the same style of CV as you would for similar job roles outside universities. If you use an academic CV for non-academic jobs, it will suggest to the university that your real desire is to be a lecturer and that you won't be committed to the job that you are applying for.

Setting out your academic CV: what to include

Personal information

Academic CVs begin much as other chronological CVs do. You should, of course, include your personal details and, if you wish, a profile.

Education

This should begin with your PhD, giving a brief summary of your thesis title, your area of research and your methodology. It is also usual to include the name of your supervisor.

Follow this with your master's degree (if you took one) and your undergraduate degree. You can include any academic scholarships, prizes or awards here if you don't have enough to justify a separate 'Awards' section.

Experience

It is helpful to break this down into sub-sections such as:

Teaching Experience

This could include running seminars, giving lectures and presentations, supervising or supporting students, demonstrating and assisting with practicals. Give a bit of background to your teaching experience, such as the course content, the level of students that you taught and the number of classes. Experience teaching in schools, tutoring or teaching English as a foreign language could also be mentioned here if your experience of teaching in higher education is still limited.

Research Experience

You can use this section to give details of any other research not covered in your PhD summary, such as postdoctoral research, year-in-industry placements that involved research, or summer schools.

Administrative Experience

Don't undervalue this experience! Academics do more than research and teaching: they also carry out administrative tasks related to areas such as exams, student recruitment and academic committees and prepare and write bids for grant funding. You can use this section to show any posts of responsibility or organisational experience.

Other professional experience

If you have worked in a role in industry, business, government, non-governmental organisations (NGOs), and so on that relates to your academic study and research you can mention it here. This could include placements, internships, consultancies or volunteering.

Other sections

Personal details, education and experience are expected on most CVs, but the following sections are usually only found on CVs for academic or research posts.

Research interests

This could be included as an alternative to 'Research Experience' if you have little experience yet outside your PhD research. Alternatively, it could be used to demonstrate how your research interests mesh with those of the department you are applying to.

Publications – books, articles, reviews, conference proceedings

This section can include journal articles, books or chapters of books, reports, book reviews and published conference papers. As in the CV as a whole, your publications should be listed in reverse chronological order. Use a recognised citation style, such as Harvard, MLA or Chicago. It doesn't usually matter which specific style you use, so you can use your department's preferred style or the style you used for your PhD bibliography, but do pick a single style and be consistent. Mixing up citation styles not only makes it harder for the reader but also looks careless.

If you already have a long list of publications, you could put them in an appendix rather than include them in the body of your CV.

Funding and awards

These could include funded studentships, awards for research projects, academic prizes or travel grants. You could include the amount of money received if this will make a strong impression.

Professional qualifications or membership of professional bodies

Only list those which are relevant to your research or to the post you are applying for, such as Chartered Physicist, Member of the Institute of Mathematics and its Applications, or barrister.

Attendance at conferences and seminars

Note whether you gave any presentations, provided posters or helped to organise a conference or seminar. As with publications, if you have taken part in a large number of conferences, you could move this section to an appendix.

Technical and other skills

Again, only include skills relevant to an academic post, such as these:

- Scientific or specialist techniques such as NMR or chromatography
- Academic and specialist IT packages such as SPSS, LexisNexis, EvaSys
- Audio-visual technology, such as lecture capture and interactive lecture tools
- Language skills

References

Three academic references are usually expected. One should be from your PhD supervisor and one from another academic who can comment on your postgraduate work. The other could be from your first degree. It may also be useful to include a reference from a current or previous employer in a relevant area, or another individual who can comment about your personal qualities as opposed to your academic performance.

What not to include

School or college education

Don't go any further back in your education section than your undergraduate degree: your earlier educational history will not be relevant at this stage.

Non-relevant work experience

You don't need to include any experience that is not relevant to academic jobs unless it demonstrates a useful skill. For example, office administration experience could be useful in an academic position but retail, bar work and babysitting should be left off your academic CV.

Interests

You don't normally need to include these on an academic CV unless they relate to your field of study and research and you haven't been able to include them elsewhere.

Example of an academic CV

The following CV shows how a graduate who has recently been awarded their PhD, and who is looking for their first full-time academic post, might set out their academic career history and achievements.

Only a couple of items have been included under the headings for Publications and Conferences Attended, to show you what you could include in these sections and how to set out this information. Even at this early stage of an academic career, a candidate might be expected to have quite a long list of items under these headings!

Dr Grant Mitchell

17 Albert Square, Walford, London E20 6PQ
G.P.Mitchell@walford.ac.uk   07700 900033

EDUCATION
2012–2016:   University of Walford
PhD in Cultural Studies
Title: 'Get outta my pub': perceptions of 'realism' and behaviour at the interface of public/private space in television serial dramas
While these dramas enact the interdependency of the domestic/private sphere (family life) and public sphere (the neighbourhood), semi-public spaces such as pubs and shops provide an ongoing setting where the boundaries of these spheres are imprecise and may fluctuate according to situation and expressed behaviours. My thesis analysed variations in text, narrative and image according to the location of the action and the impact of these upon viewers' perceptions of 'realism' and characters' behaviour in the drama. This research was conducted through the analysis of visual data and interviews with individuals to determine their reaction to, and interpretation of, representation of characters' behaviours in these differing spheres.

Supervisor: Professor Patrice Boucher
2008–2012   University of Weatherfield
2011–2012   MA in Media, Culture and Society – Distinction
Dissertation: 'Viewer responses to the representation of urban and suburban environments in television drama'
2008 – 2011   BA Sociology and Media Studies – First Class Honours
Modules included:
- Sociology of Urban Environments
- Cultural Anthropology
- Social Philosophy

AWARDS
- University Postgraduate Research Studentship 2012–2013
- CHASE AHRC funding awarded for 2013–2016
- Awarded a travel bursary from the British Institute of Cultural Studies to present a paper at the 2015 International Conference of Communication and Cultural Studies (ICCCS) conference in Adelaide, Australia
- Received the award for 'Best Student Paper' at the above ICCCS conference

EXPERIENCE
2013 to date, University of Walford
Part-time tutor in Cultural Studies and Sociology

Teaching
Taught on the following core and optional modules, devising and running lectures, seminars and practical projects

Cultural Theory
- A 24-week series of undergraduate lectures and seminars for first-year students, taught in 2015–2016. Introduced the concept of cultural studies in relation to art, media and society, drawing on the work of Foucault, Heidegger, Freud and Weber.

Sociology of Photography and Social Change
- Devised a 24-week series of seminars and project support which was offered as a special subject to final-year undergraduates in 2014–2015 and 2015–2016;
- Students learned techniques of digital photography and theories of culture to help them understand diverse cultural issues and relate these to social change;
- Supervised practical projects which facilitated students' application of these techniques and theories by enabling them to develop their own body of work and present it in the university exhibition space.

Media and Community
- A 12-week series of undergraduate lectures and seminars taught in 2013–2014 and 2014–2015. Considered aspects of broadcast media, social media, cultural identity and social interaction.

Administrative responsibilities
- Marking of essays and projects; exam preparation, invigilation and marking
- Representing the department at open days and UCAS fairs
- Organising and running visits to cultural sites and events, with responsibility for budgeting and risk assessment
- Organising exhibitions of students' work and supervising student volunteers involved in the planning and curating of these exhibitions

Other activities
- Co-organiser of the Cultural and Urban Studies Postgraduate Seminar (CUSPS): a weekend conference attended by over 100 postgraduate students from universities in the UK, France and the Netherlands
- Research Postgraduate Representative on University of Walford Arts Committee, involved in the development of the University strategy for extra-curricular arts initiatives and collaboration with the local community
- Collaborated with a local charity to offer photography workshops to homeless people and enable them to document their experiences; curated an exhibition of these photographs at Walford Arts Centre
- Member of Postgraduate Research Students' Committee

PUBLICATIONS
Journal articles
Mitchell, G. (2015) 'Urban Spaces and Places in Television Drama', *British Journal of Cultural Studies*, 12(5): 76–88.
Mitchell, G. (2015) 'Place and Perception in Television Drama', *Socio-Media Studies*, 22(9): 192–218.

Book review
Review of Cotton, N. (2014) 'Two-shot East and West: visual conventions in television drama' for *FreezeFrame Media Studies Review*, 10(2): 7–8.

Conference papers presented
British Institute of Cultural Studies Annual Conference, Salford, April 2015
'The Street, the Square and the Spaces in Between: How Text, Narrative and Image Adapt According to Location in Serial Dramas'

International Conference of Communication and Cultural Studies (ICCCS), Adelaide, Australia, January 2015
'Venue and Variation: The Impact of Setting on Viewers' Perceptions of Realism and Character in Serial Drama' Awarded 'Best Student Paper' prize

Cultural and Urban Studies Postgraduate Seminar (CUSPS), Walford, June 2014 (Co-organiser)
'[Sub]Urban Narratives and Perceptions in Serial Drama'

SKILLS AND RESEARCH TECHNIQUES
- Experienced in qualitative methods including discourse analysis and video analysis
- SPSS
- Photoshop
- Netlogo

Professional memberships
- British Institute of Cultural Studies
- International Urban Culture Society

REFERENCES
Professor Patrice Boucher, Department of Cultural Studies, University of Walford, Victoria Square, London E20 6PQ. P.Boucher@walford.ac.uk 020 7946 0988
Dr David Platt, School of Media and Cultural Studies, University of Weatherfield, Weatherfield M10 9CS D.C.S.Platt@weatherfield.ac.uk 0161 496 0159
Dr Deirdre Barlow, School of Sociology and Urban Studies, University of Weatherfield, Weatherfield M10 9CV D.H.L.Barlow@weatherfield.ac.uk 0161 496 0272

Finding out more

Applying for postgraduate study

TARGETJobs (2016) 'How to write a winning application for your postgraduate course, https://targetpostgrad.com/advice/postgraduate-applications/how-to-write-a-winning-application-for-your-postgraduate-course

FindAPhD (2016) 'Writing a Good PhD Research Proposal', https://www.findaphd.com/advice/finding/writing-phd-research-proposal.aspx

Vitae (2016) 'Writing a Research Proposal', https://www.vitae.ac.uk/doing-research/doing-a-doctorate/starting-a-doctorate/writing-a-research-proposal

Jobs.ac.uk (2016) '7 PhD Application Tips', http://www.jobs.ac.uk/careers-advice/studentships/2222/7-phd-application-tips

Applying for academic jobs

Vitae (2016) 'Creating an effective academic CV', www.vitae.ac.uk/researcher-careers/pursuing-an-academic-career/how-to-write-an-academic-cv

Jobs.ac.uk (2009) 'Academic CV Template', http://www.jobs.ac.uk/careers-advice/cv-templates/1309/academic-cv-template

Open University (2016) 'CVs for PhD researchers' http://www2.open.ac.uk/students/help/cvs-for-phd-researchers

Elsevier (2013) 'Writing an effective academic CV'. https://www.elsevier.com/connect/writing-an-effective-academic-cv

Chapter 10

International CVs

Contents

- CV conventions in different countries
- Language issues
- The Europass CV

What will you learn from this chapter?

You will learn how CV styles can vary in different countries, how to adapt your CV to use in other countries and how to describe your language skills on a CV.

How are CVs used in other countries?

Fittingly, for a document that is known in the English-speaking world by either a Latin or a French name, a CV is very international. CVs are used in almost every country of the world, under a variety of different names:

Chinese	jiǎnli
Czech	životopis
Danish	genoptag
Dutch	hervatten
Finnish	ansioluettelo
German	Lebenslauf
Indonesian	daftar riwayat hidup
Japanese	rirekisho
Polish	życiorys
Turkish	özgeçmiş

The broad structure of a CV is similar wherever it is used and the core information (personal details, education/qualifications and work experience) will be required by employers in all countries.

Don't let this fool you, though, into thinking that your CV can be used without alteration to make applications in any other country. There is really no such thing as an all-purpose 'international CV'. Different countries have different conventions on what should and should not be included in a CV and it is important to be aware of these when applying outside your own country. They may be small details, but ignoring them may mean that your CV is also ignored!

In a book of this length, it is not possible to cover every possible variation of CVs around the world, but some key differences include the following.

Photos

In many countries (such as France, Belgium and Germany), it is a requirement to include a photo of yourself on your CV. This should be a clear head-and-shoulders shot where you look smart and professional: after all, it is the first impression that you will make on the employer! Although the photo should be passport-sized, don't use your actual passport photo – a smile is allowed on a CV photo and can make all the difference. Note, though, that British and Irish employers do not usually expect a photo on your CV and that, in the USA, this is actually illegal, as it could leave employers open to charges of discrimination on ethnic background.

Length

> A candidate sent his 'Lebenslauf' to a German company, including a head-and-shoulders photo as requested. It was a good clear photo; his hair was neatly brushed and he was wearing a business suit. There was just one problem: the photo was of the back of his head. We don't know whether he was extremely shy or just being awkward, because he didn't get an interview.

In some countries, such as the USA and France, a one-page CV is an expectation rather than an option. A two-page CV will be seen as too long, so you will need to present your information much more concisely. At the other extreme, Australian CVs tend to be more personal and comprehensive and can go on for three or four pages.

Spelling

English spelling is not the same in every English-speaking country! Set your spellchecker to 'English (United States)', 'English (Australia)', and so on, as appropriate, to make sure that any variations in spelling will be picked up before they are treated as spelling mistakes.

Personal details

Employers in some countries may expect a surprising level of detail about your personal background. This can include items such as date and place of birth, religion, nationality, ethnic origin and even your parents' occupations. Check what should be included for the country that you are applying to.

References

Although the format 'References available on request' is quite normal in the United Kingdom, USA and many other countries, this would not be acceptable to a German, Swiss or Austrian employer. In these countries, you should send copies of your actual written references with your application. You should also include copies of certificates proving your educational and professional qualifications.

Presentation

Although email is normally the simplest and most obvious way to send your CV to another country, this may not always help your application.

- A Japanese *rirekisho* should traditionally be written by hand, in black ink, and be posted unfolded in an A4 or B5 envelope.
- All those references and certificates that German employers require should be presented in a plastic folder (known as *die Mappe*). You won't get this back if your application is unsuccessful so job hunting in Germany can be quite expensive!

Language issues

Many international employers ask for CVs in English: this may be the case even where the company is headquartered in Moscow and is recruiting for a hotel manager in Istanbul.

If you need to write your CV in a language other than your first language, it is more important than ever to be absolutely accurate in spelling, grammar and terminology. Online translation tools will not produce a document of sufficient quality, as the example below shows:

> 🎵This work allowed me to learn the operation of a fund and improve my speed calculation. He made me discover the importance of being attentive to the people and be proactive about their applications to represent the company well.[1] 🎵

As well as producing a rather clumsy translation, this program has translated the French word *caisse* as 'fund' rather than the more common 'cash register', giving an inaccurate picture of what the job involved.

Language skills should always be mentioned on a CV, especially for work in another country. Even if you will be working through English and don't have any knowledge of the language of the country you are applying to, showing that you can speak a language other than your own demonstrates your ability to learn.

You should give an indication of your competency in the language. Never exaggerate your ability: if you state that you are 'fluent' in another language, an employer might decide to conduct the interview in that language!

There is no standard format for evaluating language competency, but the following rough guide may be helpful:

- **'Native speaker'** means that you have spoken this language throughout your life.
- **'Bilingual'** implies that you speak two languages at native speaker level.
- **'Fluent'** implies that you can easily hold a complex conversation but are not a native speaker.
- **'Conversational'** suggests you can have a conversation on common everyday topics.
- **'Reading'** suggests that you can read a reasonably complex piece of text (such as a newspaper article) but may not be so readily able to take part in a conversation.
- **'Basic knowledge'** suggests you know enough of the language to get by on holiday.

A more structured and detailed format is the Common European Framework of Reference for Languages (CEFR) which sets out and describes six levels of competency. The CEFR framework is included in the 'Europass

CV', http://europass.cedefop.europa.eu/en/resources/european-language-levels-cefr/cef-ell-document.pdf.

The Europass CV

This document was introduced in the late 1990s with the aim of helping people to make their qualifications and competences clearly understood in EU member states and therefore to facilitate mobility of work and study throughout Europe. The Europass CV is now one of a set of five documents in which you can set out your language skills, educational and vocational qualifications and record any organised period of work or training in another country, such as an internship or a year abroad as part of your degree. It is quite similar to an application form, with sections for personal details, work experience, education and training, skills and so on. You can download a copy from https://europass.cedefop.europa.eu/.

Although the Europass CV has now been around for almost 20 years, it has never really caught on with employers. Many employers actively dislike it, finding it unclear, poorly structured and providing only quite basic information which does not allow candidates to put themselves over as individuals. In general, we would not recommend using this format unless the employer specifically asks for it or, possibly, to apply for one of the European institutions (and even here, not all of these institutions will use the Europass CV, so check before you apply).

'I am a citizen of the European Onion.'

–Real quote from a student CV

Finding out more

JobERA (2016) *International CVs Writing Guide*, http://jobera.com/cvs-worldwide/international-cvs.html

TARGETJobs (2016) *Working Abroad*, https://targetjobs.co.uk/careers-advice/working-abroad Job search and application advice for 40 countries.

Eurograduate (2014) *Are you ready to work in Europe?* http://www. eurograduate.com/planning.asp. Advice on presenting your CV in various European countries.

Going Global https://online.goinglobal.com. This is a career and employment resource which includes worldwide job and internship vacancies, industry profiles, advice on CV/resume preparation and country-specific career information. It is a subscription-based site but your university careers service may be able to provide access to it.

References

1. Original version : *Ce travail m'a permis d'apprendre le fonctionnement d'une caisse et d'améliorer ma rapidité de calcul. Il m'a fait découvrir l'importance d'être à l'écoute des gens et d'être proactif face à leurs demandes pour bien représenter la compagnie.* (https://www.caissealliance.com/fr/jeunesse/recherche-demploi/modele-de-curriculum-vitae/).

Chapter 11

Video CVs

What will you learn from this chapter?

You will learn the difference between a video CV and a normal CV, when video CVs should be used, the positives and negatives of video CVs and how to produce one.

What is a video CV?

In a video CV, you produce a short video to sell yourself to recruiters. Video CVs are becoming popular with students who wish to stand out from the crowd, and an increasing number of graduate recruiters are building these into their graduate recruitment programmes. Video CVs don't replace standard CVs, but instead enhance your CV by giving employers an insight into your personality. They show your presentation skills but can be used whenever you want to make an impact. Just preparing a video CV shows the employer you are prepared to go the extra mile. It's simply another tool: anything that helps you to get noticed is worth trying. Recruiters are intrigued to see video CVs as they are still relatively new and communicate your personality visually.

According to a survey by Kloodle,[1] a social networking site for graduate recruitment, UK students think that video CVs are more dynamic than traditional CVs and better showcase their skills. It found that although 57 per cent of the students surveyed were still comfortable with using the traditional approach to job hunting, 42 per cent were ready to use more modern techniques, and 44 per cent said an online format with video content and images appealed to them most.

When should you use a video CV?

Whether you use a video CV depends on the sector, the role you're applying for and your personality. They are most useful when applying for creative or customer-facing roles in sales, the media, marketing, PR and advertising.

> One candidate created a rap video CV on YouTube to land a job with an architecture firm known for its creativity.

How often are video CVs used?

Use of video CVs has greatly increased as they are now easily produced. Most phones and laptops now have high resolution cameras to allow production of high quality videos. The site Video Recruit[2] allows users to create recruitment profiles with or without video, and it found that profiles with a video CV are clicked on seven times more frequently than those without.

How long should a video CV last?

They work best when one to three minutes long – keep it short and engaging. At a typical talking speed of 130 words per minute, a video CV might contain around 300 words.

Body language and clothing

Dress as for an interview. Wear a suit for a formal role, but wear smart casual clothes if the job is more relaxed and creative. Maintain eye contact with the camera – and smile!

Example video CV script

| Introduce yourself clearly: you only have a few seconds to engage the viewer. | *I'm Kirsty Jones, a final year History student at the University of Stirling, and I'm looking for a job in digital marketing.* |

Say why you wish to work in the career and why you're the right person for the job. It's your chance to inject personality into your application and show your communication skills, professionalism and passion for the job. List your strengths and relevant experience.	*My interest in marketing started when I became publicity officer for the university Hogwarts Society, where I publicised events via Facebook and Twitter and helped to increase membership by 25 per cent. Last summer I undertook a work experience placement with a small digital marketing agency in Birmingham, where I maintained the social media presence of several clients and wrote web content, which confirmed my passion for this area.*
Put across three or four key selling points such as a relevant degree, good grades, relevant work experience, strong achievements or job-related skills. You could also add your interests or an interesting fact to help you stand out from the crowd.	*Whilst studying, I've successfully combined my studies with work and other commitments. I have a drive to see things through to completion, and I try to learn something new from every experience because I believe there's always room for self-improvement.* *I have successfully completed the European Computer Driving Licence, which has greatly improved my computing skills.*
Include your contact details.	Your email, LinkedIn, Twitter, website or blog.
End by thanking the viewer.	*Thank you for taking the time to view my video CV.*

Now write your own script

Introduce yourself clearly.

Say why you wish to work in the career and why you're the right person for the job.

> Think of three or four key selling points to put across.

> Include your contact details and end by thanking the viewer.

Now record yourself reading your script on your phone. How long did it last? Did you sound confident and fluent? Show it to a friend to get another opinion. This won't be your final, polished version, but will get you started.

Negatives of video CVs

With a video CV, social class, ethnicity, weight, age and sex can all be determined, so some organisations dislike them as they increase the possibility of discrimination. One experiment[3] found that agreeableness was rated higher, but extraversion, social skills and mental capability were rated lower on average in video CVs compared to paper CVs.

Video CVs give employers a great chance to reject you before you've even met, so only produce a video CV if you think you have something special to offer and you can put this across on video.

> One candidate changed into different clothes during his video CV to show his adaptability.

How to use your video CV

You can post your CV online for free on sites such as YouTube, Vimeo, Vine, Instagram or your blog, or on specialist sites such as Video Recruit and Kloodle. Share it to get as many views as possible. Add a link from your LinkedIn profile.

Send it to companies you would like to work for, but be careful of sending it to more traditional organisations who might not appreciate this type of approach.

Video CV checklist

Video CVs come in many formats, allowing you to express your individuality. There are no set rules for creating one, but here are some ideas.

❏ **Write your script in advance.** Make a list of your unique selling points: the attributes that make you a strong candidate.

❏ **Research the business** that you are applying to, and personalise the video to it. Demonstrate your passion for the industry you wish to work in.

❏ **Choose your location carefully:** a quiet, private room. Don't film in a dark environment.

❏ **Make sure that the viewer will not be distracted by anything in the background** such as tatty posters or an unmade bed. Focus your camera on your face, not the background.

❏ **Sit at a desk or table** rather than in an armchair or on the bed. You will appear more professional as you will be sitting up straight rather than slouching.

❏ **Dress as for a face-to-face interview** as this will make you feel more confident. You could, however, wear your pyjama bottoms if these are out of view!

❏ **Don't do anything you wouldn't do in an interview.** Approach recording your video CV just as you would a face-to-face meeting.

❏ **Practise.** Record yourself to see how you appear on camera. Be aware of your surroundings and the lighting.

❏ **Point the webcam at your face and shoulders.** Use a laptop for the final version, rather than your phone, for a stable image, or you could use a GoPro or, for high quality, a DSLR camera.

❏ **If you have technical skills** such as Adobe After Effects, you can demonstrate these and make your video more interesting by adding photos, animations and text, but don't let these dominate the CV.

❏ **Look at the camera**, not down at the desk, so it looks like you are talking directly to the employer.

❏ **Have your script 'off camera'** to refer to while recording your video. Sticky notes next to the webcam work well. It is obvious if you look away from the camera to read notes. Try to memorise your script, if possible, as you will look and sound less stilted than if you are reading it from a prompt.

❑ **Initial presentation is vital,** so be positive and smile! Relax and talk clearly and confidently.

A French student stuck a QR code on his CV, which, when scanned by a phone, streamed his video CV. He got several job offers when the video went viral.

Finding out more

Video: what to do and what not to do when filming your video CV, www. inspiringinterns.com/candidates/how-it-works/video-cv-tips.

References

1. Kloodle (www.kloodle.com) social networking site for student and graduate employability.
2. Video Recruit (www.video-recruit.com) allows candidates to record an automated online video.
3. Waung, M., Hymes R. and Beatty J. (2014) 'The Effects of Video and Paper Resumes on Assessments of Personality, Applied Social Skills, Mental Capability, and Resume Outcomes', Basic and Applied Social Psychology, 36(3), 238–51, http://dx.doi.org/10.1080/01973533.2014.894477.

Covering letters

Contents

What will you learn from this chapter?

You will learn how to write an effective covering letter, how to set out your letter and what to include in it.

What is a covering letter?

A covering letter builds on the brief, factual information in the CV, to give the employer some further details of your experience, skills and motivation.

You can also use it to explain anything in your application that could potentially disadvantage you, such as poor exam results or gaps in your career history.

It may be sent on paper, as an electronic document, or as the text of an email message to which your CV is attached.

When should you use a covering letter?

With just one or two exceptions, you should always send a covering letter with your CV. Without it, your CV is incomplete and you are missing out on a real opportunity to sell yourself to the employer. A covering letter is a vital part of your application: it adds depth to the factual information outlined in your CV and highlights those parts of the CV that will be of most interest and relevance to the employer.

The only times when it would _not_ be a good idea to send a covering letter are:

- if an employer specifically says 'no covering letters'.
- if you are uploading your CV to attach to an online application form.
- if you are uploading your CV to a recruitment site where it may be seen by multiple employers.

What should you include in a covering letter?

A good framework is as follows:

- Introduce yourself: give a brief outline of who you are and what you are applying for.
- Say why you are applying for the job – what interests you about that employer and that job?
- Say what you can bring to the job – why they should choose you.
- The final paragraph should give any practical information that may be relevant, such as when you would be available for interview or to start work, and finish with a polite and positive phrase such as 'I look forward to hearing from you'.

How long should a covering letter be?

Keep it brief: not more than three or four paragraphs. If your covering letter is printed out, it should cover no more than one side of A4 paper.

Covering letter framework

Your address **1**

Date

Name of recipient

Their address **2**

Dear . . ., **3**

Introduction:

What job are you applying for? **4**

Where did you see it advertised? **5**

About yourself: what can you bring to the job?

Give some detail about the education, experience and/or skills that you can offer that will be of **6**
most interest to this employer.

About yourself: what interests you about this job and/or this employer?

Say something that you could not say to any other employer. Show that you have done the
research outlined in Chapter 4.

Conclusion:

This could include information about your availability for interview and any attached documents.
Otherwise, end with polite thanks and a positive reinforcement of your sign off as below:

Thank you for considering my application. I hope that you feel that my skills and experience
make me a suitable candidate for this position and I look forward to hearing from you.

Yours sincerely/Yours faithfully, **7**

Signature

Print your name below your signature.

Notes

1. Your covering letter should include these addresses and the date if you are sending it by post or as a document attached to an email. Some style guides suggest putting your address and the date at the left margin along with the employer's address and the letter itself: this is possible but placing them on the right improves the visual appearance of the letter. If, though, you are using the email text box for your covering letter you don't need these.

2. As above, but the employer's name and address should always be in this position.

3. Use a personal name if you have one, for example 'Dear Mr Singh'; otherwise use 'Dear Sir or Madam'.

4. The employer may be recruiting for several jobs, so give the exact job title and the reference number if there is one.

5. Recruiters like to know that the money they spend on advertising vacancies is being used effectively, so give the name of the publication or website where you saw this job.

6. Motivation and enthusiasm are important – show that you are really interested in this job and this employer.

7. 'Yours sincerely' if you have started with a name and 'Yours faithfully' if you have started with 'Dear Sir or Madam'.

Exercise: now use this framework to draft a covering letter of your own.

How to start your letter – and how not to

When you know the recipient's name	
Dear Ms Bloggs	✓
Dear Mrs/Miss Bloggs	✗
Dear Lucy Bloggs	✗
Dear Ms Lucy Bloggs	✗
Dear Lucy	✗
Hi Lucy	✗

When you don't know the recipient's name	
Dear Sir or Madam	✓
Dear Human Resources Manager	✓
Dear Graduate Recruitment Team	✓
Dear Sirs	✗
To Whom It May Concern	✗
Hi	✗

How to end your letter

When you know the recipient's name
Yours sincerely
When you don't know the recipient's name
Yours faithfully

These are the *only* ways in which you should sign off a business letter: phrases such as 'Kind regards' or 'Best wishes' or single words such as 'Yours', 'Sincerely' or 'Cheers' are not appropriate in these letters.

What makes a good covering letter?

- It is aimed at one particular job and employer. Each covering letter should be unique and carefully targeted at the specific job you are applying for.
- It complements and expands on the CV, adding further information and detail rather than repeating it.
- It relates to the job description and person specification (where available), highlighting the skills, experience and qualifications that make you a good candidate for this job (see Chapter 4).
- It shows your motivation and enthusiasm.
- It is written in clear and accurate English. Your covering letter demonstrates your written communication skills and attention to detail; any errors in spelling and grammar, or a clumsy writing style, could mean instant rejection.
- It answers the question 'Why should I choose you? What can you offer me?'
- It should make the employer want to meet you!

Dos and don'ts for covering letters

- *Do* make it interesting to read.
- *Do* say why you want to work for that employer.
- *Don't* make your letter too long.
- *Don't* use tired, hackneyed phrases or over-elaborate vocabulary.
- *Do* use the advice given in this chapter – but *don't* quote paragraphs and phrases from the example letters directly. Use your own words to write your letter.

Covering letter examples

How *not* to write a covering letter

Dear Sirs,   1

I am keen to join _____ (*space to insert the company name*)_____ to work as a   2
_____ (*another space to insert the job title*) _____ as you are a highly reputable   3
employer that any graduate would be proud to work for.

I also would like a career where I can work in another country and as a prestigous global   4
company _____ (*space to insert the company name*) offers me the chance to do   5
this.

I am sure that my academic achievements and my enthusiasm for _____ (*space to insert*   6
the job role) make me a uniquely ideal candidate for _____ (*space to insert the company*   7
name) and I look forward to being able to quickly make a notable contribution to your success.

Hope to hear from you soon.   8

Best

Frank

This letter is based on one used almost 100 times by a real student, who finally sought advice from his careers service as to why he had never heard back from any of the employers to whom he had sent it. Here are just some of the reasons:

1. If the reader is a woman, Frank has already got off to a bad start by addressing her as 'Dear Sirs'.
2. A 'fill the gaps' letter such as this is not only lazy but also runs the risk that you will miss one of these insertions when adapting the letter for the next employer, thus telling BP that you are an ideal candidate for Shell, or vice versa.
3. Words such as 'reputable' are meaningless in job applications. You wouldn't want to apply to a 'disreputable' company, would you?
4. This suggests that Frank only wants to join a global company for the travel opportunities. He doesn't mention anything such as language skills or study abroad that might make him useful to an international company.
5. Any spellchecker would tell Frank that it is 'prestigious' not 'prestigous'.
6. This letter does not exactly demonstrate any enthusiasm!
7. 'Unique' is probably overstating his case. Although you shouldn't be over-modest in your applications, don't go to the other extreme and come over as arrogant – especially where you can't give any evidence to back up these claims.
8. 'Hope to hear from you' and 'Best' are both too casual for the conclusion of a business letter.

Once Frank realised that he had to put time and effort into his cover letters, research employers, match his skills to the job and demonstrate his abilities and enthusiasm, he began to get interviews. The covering letters on the following pages give examples of how it should be done!

Summer Placement Student: ref MGH/CLS/354

You will assist Biomedical Scientists and be responsible for the reception and sample processing of specimens, along with core departmental laboratory assistant duties.

This post will involve receiving specimens from patients and entering information into the laboratory computer system. The placement student will also assist in the testing of samples.

Good communication skills together with an excellent telephone manner are essential requirements for this post, together with the ability to work as part of a team.

Apply with CV to Matilda Jenkyns, HR Manager

8 Russell Street
Manchester
M37 2JK

12 April 2017

Ms Matilda Jenkyns   **1**
Human Resources Manager
Manchester General Hospital
Manchester
M39 5BJ

Dear Ms Jenkyns,   **2**

I am writing to apply for the placement in the Clinical Laboratory Sciences Department   **3**
(ref. MGH/CLS/354) advertised through the University of Bath Careers Service. I have a
strong interest in laboratory procedures and clinical diagnostics which first began after a   **4**
school visit to your laboratories where I was fascinated to see the differing techniques used
in testing clinical samples for patients. The opportunity that this placement offers to gain
hands-on experience in your leading Clinical Laboratory Sciences department is therefore
very exciting for me.

My degree course has developed my laboratory and computing skills, and given me experience   **5**
of using several diagnostic tests. I achieved 68% in my first-year examinations and expect a
high 2.1 for my course project this year. While at University, I have worked part-time at a busy
insurance telephone helpline, which has taught me the importance of listening to customers,   **6**
giving clear and accurate information and supporting co-workers.

I will be available for interview at any time and would be able to take up the placement from
5 June onwards. I enclose my CV giving further information and look forward to hearing from you.   **7**

Yours sincerely,   **8**

Rosalind Franklin

Rosalind Franklin

1. The sender's and recipient's addresses are placed at the start of the letter.
2. The letter is addressed to a named person, using the format 'Dear Ms Jenkyns' – not 'Dear Matilda' or 'Dear Ms Matilda Jenkyns'.
3. This letter has been sent in response to an advertised job (see the box on page 141), so Rosalind starts by giving the reference number and saying where she saw it advertised.
4. The letter shows motivation by mentioning previous contact with this area of work (in this case, with this actual employer).
5. It mentions relevant laboratory and computing skills gained through her studies and highlights her good academic results.
6. The letter uses experience from outside science to show the required communication, telephone and teamworking skills.
7. The final paragraph gives practical information on availability for interview and to start work before referring the reader to her CV and ending with a pleasant and positive 'I look forward to hearing from you'.
8. Having started with the recipient's name, this letter ends 'Yours sincerely'.

Are you passionate about food and working in the food industry? Do you have experience of working in a fast paced environment?

PearLait, a multinational dairy products company, is looking for a bright, motivated Graduate Procurement Trainee to help buy in the top-quality raw materials that go into our renowned brands.

You should have excellent academic qualifications (320 UCAS points and a 2.1 degree in a Business or Food related subject) with some experience of working in a fast-paced environment such as retail or food/drink manufacturing. You need to be good with numbers, have excellent communication skills and be creative, commercially aware and able to take the initiative.

Send a CV and letter showing us how you meet these requirements to tariq.mahir@pearlait.com quoting ref. GPT/16/113.

To: tariq.mahir@pearlait.com

From: millie29@kambaros.net   1

Subject: Graduate Procurement Trainee application ref. GPT/16/113

Dear Mr Mahir,

I am writing to apply for the Graduate Procurement Trainee position (ref. GPT/16/113) advertised   2
on Milkround.com.

I am interested in Procurement as a career which will combine the analytical and numerical
skills I have developed through my Business degree with my interest in food. As an assistant   3
restaurant manager, I helped to manage stock, source local suppliers and build relationships with
them. This was a varied role in a fast-paced environment which demanded creativity and strong
business awareness and which I found highly enjoyable.

From reading the graduate profiles on your recruitment website, I feel that your Procurement
programme would offer me the same interest and job satisfaction. PearLait's reputation for   4
innovative and high-quality dairy products, such as your new range of savoury yoghurts, proves
your consistent drive for excellence and commitment to development.

 During my A Levels, I suffered mild concussion in a road accident the day before I was due to sit   5
two papers. This affected my revision and concentration, and I achieved 300 UCAS points rather
than the 340 predicted. However, I was still accepted onto my chosen course and have achieved
high grades ever since.

I attach my CV and hope that it will persuade you of my potential to make a real contribution as
a member of the PearLait team. Thank you for your consideration and I look forward to hearing
from you.

Yours sincerely,

Millie Kambaros

1. This 'covering letter' is designed to be sent as the text of an email and so does not include addresses or date at the top. In the subject line, give the job title and any reference number.
2. The letter sets out what she is applying for (companies often recruit graduates into several different functions) and says where she saw the vacancy advertised.
3. It gives her motivation for applying, some further detail of her relevant experience, the skills she can offer and generally shows enthusiasm.
4. This paragraph shows that she has not just looked at the company website but says what she has found interesting and displays a knowledge of their products.
5. This paragraph is the crunch point and could make all the difference to this application. On paper, Millie would not meet the basic requirements of a company that asks for 320 UCAS points; however, there are mitigating circumstances to her A-level grades, which she sets out briefly. She also ends on a positive note by highlighting the high grades that she has achieved at University and showing her enthusiasm for the job.

Speculative covering letters: when you don't know exactly what job you are applying for

The previous covering letters have been tailored to meet the requirements set out in job advertisements. Often, though, you will want to use your covering letter to make a speculative application – one based on the hope that the employer will have opportunities even though they aren't actually advertising any! Research indicates that anything from 60–80 per cent of jobs are never advertised, so speculative applications are an important job-hunting tactic.

To: Geraldine.Maguire@sportpromo.co.uk   1
From: vijay97@arjuna.net
Subject: Enquiry about work experience opportunities

Dear Ms Maguire,

I am a second-year Business and Marketing student at the University of East Anglia and am   2
contacting you to ask if you may have any work experience opportunities at SportProMo this
summer.

I am keen to start a career in sports marketing, as it combines my degree knowledge with my   3
passion for sport and my strong communication and organisational skills. I am secretary of   4
the university Archery Club and over the last year have increased membership from 30 to 120
students through 'have a go' sessions, social media and linking up with other student societies.

As well as demonstrating my ability to market and promote the club in the face of strong
competition from better-established sports, this has developed my organisational and   5
administrative skills, as I have had to keep accurate records, liaise with the Sports Federation
and ensure safety at all activities.

I am particularly keen to gain experience at SportsProMo as you work with clients across a wide
range of sports and associated businesses. I am a member of 'Ful Fans Ahead', the online fan   6
zone that you created for Fulchester United, which has achieved enormous popularity among
fans by using diverse social media channels and activities to engage fans of all ages, thus
consolidating the club's brand and increasing marketing opportunities.

I attach my CV and hope that my experience, enthusiasm and strong work ethic will convince   7
you to give me a chance at SportProMo this summer. I will be available at any time from 20 June
until 7 September.

Yours sincerely,

Vijay Arjuna

Speculative applications should follow the same framework as that set out on page 136: introduce yourself, say what you are looking for and what you can offer and show your motivation and enthusiasm. This is even more important when the employer is not actively trying to fill a vacancy at the moment: you need to give them a reason to read your letter. Keep it brief and to the point.

1. Find an appropriate person to address the letter to. The head of HR may not always be the right person: the head of the department or function you want to work in is the one that you want to impress.
2. Say who you are and what you are looking for. Keep this as open as you can without looking unfocused: if you ask for something very specific such as 'a three-month internship during the summer vacation' an employer may feel unable to commit to this. 'Work experience' is a much broader term and could cover anything from a week's observation to a longer work placement.
3. Say why you are interested in this type of work – you can use this to sell yourself as well as just saying what you are looking for.
4. This shows what he has achieved in this role and how he went about it.
5. Vijay also demonstrates his ability to work accurately and carry out more routine tasks – important in almost any job role.
6. This demonstrates first-hand knowledge of the employer and an awareness of what this marketing initiative aims to achieve.
7. The letter ends on a positive note and provides specific information.

Researching employers and jobs is even more important for speculative applications than for advertised jobs. If your application doesn't show an understanding of the job role that you want, your suitability for it, and your knowledge of that employer, the employer will have no reason to consider creating an opening for you.

How to send a covering letter

Most covering letters will be sent by email, along with the CV. It works best if you put the text of your covering letter in the body of the email and then attach your CV as a Word or PDF document. By doing this, the employer will be able to read your letter as soon as they open your email and will then hopefully be impressed enough to open your attached CV. An email that says no more than 'Please find attached my CV and covering letter for the position of . . .' will not have the same impact!

Whatever you do, don't forget to attach your CV!

Printing out your CV and covering letter to send by post or deliver by hand is uncommon but its rarity value may just help to get you noticed. Use good-quality paper and, ideally, an A4 size envelope so that you don't need to fold your CV. Note that Royal Mail classes this size of envelope as a 'large letter', so postage will be more expensive. Make sure that you use the right stamp – an employer will not be impressed if they have to pay excess postage!

Some real quotes from covering letters:

- I was working for my mother until she decided to move.
- Working in a chip shop developed my customer service skills in a fat moving environment.
- I have a full, clean driving licence and my own cat.
- Here are my qualifications for you to overlook.
- I am accustomed to taking responsibility, having been head bog at school.
- I used to compete in show-jumping competitions on my horse, from which I got a real kick.

Quiz to test what you have learned

1. You should always send a covering letter with your CV.
   (A) TRUE   **(B)** FALSE   **(C)** PERHAPS
2. A covering letter should be no longer than four paragraphs.
   (A) TRUE   **(B)** FALSE   **(C)** PERHAPS
3. If your letter starts with 'Dear Sir or Madam' it should end with 'Yours sincerely'.
   (A) TRUE   **(B)** FALSE   **(C)** PERHAPS
4. You can use the same covering letter for all your applications to similar jobs by just changing the name of the company.
   (A) TRUE   **(B)** FALSE   **(C)** PERHAPS
5. A covering letter should be sent by post, not email.
   (A) TRUE   **(B)** FALSE   **(C)** PERHAPS

6. You should put both your own address and the recipient's address at the top of your covering letter.
   (A) TRUE   **(B)** FALSE   **(C)** PERHAPS
7. You should never mention anything negative about yourself, such as poor exam grades, in a covering letter.
   (A) TRUE   **(B)** FALSE   **(C)** PERHAPS
8. You should tell an employer as much as you can about yourself in a covering letter.
   (A) TRUE   **(B)** FALSE   **(C)** PERHAPS

Finding out more

Prospects (2015) *Cover letters* www.prospects.ac.uk/careers-advice/cvs-and-cover-letters/cover-letters

Innes, J. (2015) *The Cover Letter Book: How to Write a Winning Cover Letter That Really Gets Noticed*, 3rd edn (Harlow: Pearson Education Ltd).

Quiz answers

1. (A) TRUE – unless you are uploading it to go with an application form, or the employer has asked you not to send one.

2. (A) TRUE. This works out to about one side of A4.

3. (B) FALSE. You should use 'Yours faithfully' here.

4. (B) FALSE. Absolutely not: a covering letter should always be targeted on a specific job and employer.

5. (B) FALSE. Email is the normal way to send a covering letter. There is nothing wrong with sending your CV and letter by post, but it will work out to be quite expensive!

6. (A) TRUE – unless you are sending your covering letter as the text of an email.

7. (B) FALSE. You can use the covering letter to tell the story behind these and persuade the employer that you are still a good candidate.

8. (B) FALSE. Keep the letter brief and leave the employer with something to find out at interview.

Chapter 13

Mind the gap – and other CV problems

Contents

What will you learn from this chapter?

You will learn how to present gaps in your career history on your CV; how to deal with issues such as illness, disabilities and poor academic grades; and how mature students and graduates can present their life experience on a CV.

Introduction

There may be something in your career history that you feel will be difficult to put over on your CV. This could be time out for health reasons or family responsibilities; it could be dropping out of a course and starting afresh; it could be poor exam results or periods of unemployment. So how do you explain issues like these on your CV – or should you mention them at all?

Well, it can be easier to deal with some of these issues on a CV than on an application form. Application forms are often set out with compulsory sections that demand full details of exams taken (with dates and grades – some forms even say, 'List all exams taken, including failures') and a full career history of employers, dates and reasons for leaving. CVs have greater flexibility.

Remember that a CV is your document and you can put in or leave out, within reason, whatever you want. It is flexible, but always be truthful in what you do put in. You must tell the truth – but not necessarily the whole truth.

It is better to deal with issues such as disability, illness and other health-related issues, family responsibilities, convictions and so on in your covering letter rather than your CV. This allows you to give background to the 'problem', show how you have managed it and what you have learned or achieved through it or despite it. However, sometimes these issues may cause problems when setting out your CV.

Every case is individual and there is no right or wrong approach. You should consult a careers adviser or other expert if possible. However, these may be issues that worry you more than they will worry potential employers. Presenting them in a straightforward way, without evasion or apology, is better than leaving gaps unaccounted for or withholding information.

Gaps

One of the main concerns for many graduates is how to explain gaps in their career history. These gaps may be due to ill-health, unemployment, changes in course, time out or family responsibilities.

How you set out your CV can influence the effect that these gaps may have on employers. A chronological CV makes gaps obvious, while a skills-based CV minimises them.

There may be times, though, when it will help your application to explain these gaps briefly on your CV. This chapter looks at some of the ways in which you could go about this.

Gaps in your education

Graduate recruiters are aware that a standard degree from an English or Welsh university, without a placement year or a year abroad, usually lasts three years and will be curious as to why someone has taken longer than this. If you had to take time out for your degree for any reason, such as illness, it is helpful to note this briefly on your CV as below:

> **2010–2015, University of Lincoln**
> **BSc (Hons) Psychology class 2.1**
>
> **Modules included:**
> Developmental Psychology; Organisational Psychology; Psychology at Work; Mental Health & Psychology; Addictions; Social Psychology; Psychopharmacology; Cross-Cultural Psychology
>
> I took a year out from this degree after my second year to support my mother, who has multiple sclerosis, and returned to University in 2013 to finish my studies as a part-time student.

You can then use the covering letter to give more background to this gap if you wish:

> As you will see from my CV, I intermitted from my degree for a year between 2012–2013 when my mother developed speech and mobility difficulties due to MS. I helped to provide day-to-day care and transport, and liaised with medical and social care services. I then returned to my studies on a part-time basis while continuing to provide support as needed. This experience developed my ability to plan and organise my time and to liaise with a variety of professionals in the healthcare system, including counsellors and psychologists.

Changes in degree course or university should also be noted briefly on your CV, unless you withdrew from a course after only a few weeks:

> **2015 to date   Imperial College London BSc Geology**
>
> **2014   University of Bristol**
>
> Completed the first term of BSc Mathematics and Physics with a grade of 64% before withdrawing from this course in order to transfer to Imperial College.

Your covering letter can then outline the reasons for your decision to change course and the benefits that you feel you have gained from this change. There is no need to excuse yourself or to go into too much detail: changing direction in this way, rather than drifting on in a course of study that is not right for you, shows strength of character and decisiveness.

> During my studies at school and college, my best subjects were maths and physics and I was delighted when I was offered a place to study these subjects at Bristol. Although I did well on the course, I found the approach to these subjects at degree level was more theoretical and less practical than really appealed to me. I therefore took the difficult decision to withdraw from Bristol at the end of the first year to study Geology, which I have found much more relevant and interesting. I feel that my year studying maths and physics has given me a solid theoretical foundation which has benefited my studies in Geology.

What if you failed a course or had to repeat exams?

You can use a similar approach to the examples above. Keep this information brief on the CV but be prepared to go into more detail on the covering letter or at interview:

> **2014 – 2105   University of Bristol**
>
> Completed the first year of study for a BSc in Mathematics and Physics
>
> I experienced personal difficulties during my second year and was disappointed to fail my exams at the end of this year. I was determined to continue my studies even though this meant changing course and university. After this, I coped much better, as shown by the good grades that I achieved.

If you had to resit any exams, you don't need to mention this on your CV but, if you had to repeat a year, it will obviously mean that the dates for your degree will appear a year longer than usual. As mentioned, graduate recruiters will notice this, although companies that don't regularly recruit graduates may not be so familiar with the structure of different degrees. In this situation, it may be better to give brief reasons for the extra year in your covering letter.

There is no need to include the first set of results for any exams that you had to repeat on your CV.

Gaps in your employment history

Gap years

If you took a gap year between school and university, or after university, to work or travel, you don't need to worry about this. This is common enough for you to be able to include on your CV without needing to explain your reasons for taking a gap year. You should, though, say something about your activities during this time, either by giving details of the jobs or volunteering you did or by giving a summary. Don't just list the countries that you visited but say a bit about what you did there and/or what you learned.

January – May 2015

Travelled independently to Thailand, Vietnam, Cambodia, Laos and Malaysia. This experience developed my planning, budgeting and problem-solving skills and gave me an insight into different cultures.

A gap year doesn't have to have involved travelling through three continents or helping to build a school in a remote Himalayan village to benefit your CV. If you have had to work in a shop, restaurant, office or building site to help fund your studies, this will be equally valuable evidence of your skills.

'One of the best CVs I have seen came from a student who spent his gap year volunteering in a hostel for homeless people with drug and alcohol problems in Glasgow. He used this experience to show his adaptability, communication and problem-solving skills, resilience and commitment, and I felt that if he could cope with this he could cope with anything!'

Recruitment partner in a City law firm

Gaps due to illness or unemployment

These can be harder to explain, but you may not need to. If the gap is quite short, you can cover it by giving dates as full years rather than months, for example '2015' rather than 'March–July 2015'.

If the gap lasted for a year or more, or you have only very short periods of employment within a period of time, it is better not to try to hide this gap but to say something about what you were doing during that time and how you used it constructively. Even if these activities only took up a minor part of your time, including them shows that you were doing something and making the most of your time. Present any volunteering or study as professionally as possible: this shows that you took it seriously and helps it blend into the rest of your CV:

2014 – 2015 Classroom Helper, Vale Primary School, Cardiff

- Assisted teachers to prepare lesson materials.
- Listened to children reading.
- Helped children with maths and English exercises.
- Accompanied teachers and children on outings.
- Gained an insight into the curriculum and class management.

Note that you don't *have* to declare that this experience was part-time, voluntary or whether you obtained it because your mum worked at the school or your children attended it. None of this is as important as what you did and what you learned.

2015–2016

Independent home study during intermission from University

- Kept up with general reading related to my degree course.
- Developed practical IT skills, including web design.

Should I mention disability or health issues on my CV?

In general, there is absolutely no need to mention any illness or disability on your CV for its own sake. If these issues don't affect your ability to do the job in any way, there is not normally any reason to mention them either in your application or at interview.

If, though, any significant gaps on your CV are due to health problems, then you may need to give these as a reason. If you are no longer affected by these problems, reassure the employer of this.

> Following a serious road accident, in which I suffered a fractured pelvis and other injuries, I was unable to work for eight months. I am now fully recovered and physically able to undertake the duties that this job requires.

This is fine, but what if you have an ongoing health problem or disability?

The Equality Act 2010 defines disability as 'a physical or mental impairment that has a substantial and long-term negative effect on your ability to do normal daily activities'. As well as physical impairments, such as mobility difficulties, sensory impairments, such as those affecting sight and hearing, and specific learning difficulties such as dyslexia, the Act also covers mental health conditions and 'hidden' disorders such as asthma and diabetes.

Deciding whether or not to mention an illness or disability on your CV is not easy. Some employers operate a scheme which guarantees an interview to disabled applicants who meet the minimum criteria for the role they have applied for, so in this situation your disability could have a positive part to play in the application process.

Many applicants, though, are wary of disclosing any information which they feel might prejudice employers against them. Although discrimination on the grounds of any condition covered under the Equality Act 2010 is, of course, illegal, this is still a common fear, especially among people with a condition that they feel is often misunderstood, such as mental illness or HIV.

Although, as said, there is no obligation for you to say anything about any illness or disability on your CV, there may be situations when you have only two options: to disclose or to leave an unexplained gap. If you decide that disclosing is the lesser of two evils, use your covering letter to present your medical history or disability as positively as possible. Showing how it helped you develop skills such as determination to overcome challenges or find creative solutions to problems is one way to do this. Be brief and don't let the issue dominate your application.

> *I withdrew from my first degree course due to depression. For a year I was unable to work or study but focused on developing strategies for dealing with my condition and then spent the following year building up my skills and confidence through part-time study and volunteering on conservation projects. I was then able to return to university to start another degree and, although I experienced further depressive episodes during this course, I was able to manage them and to successfully complete my degree.*

Mature students and graduates

As well as gaps for childcare and family reasons, mature students may face other problems when constructing a graduate CV, such as:

How much information should you include about qualifications you gained a long time ago?

You may not need to mention these qualifications on your CV at all. Some GCSE subjects (normally maths and English) may be a requirement in certain career areas, such as teaching or accountancy, but otherwise you can just mention the qualifications that got you into your degree course, whether these were A Levels, an Access course or a foundation course.

How can you condense many different jobs into two pages?

You don't need to list every single job you have ever done: most employers will not expect you to go back more than ten years. Obviously, even ten years is quite a long time, and many people will have done a lot of different jobs over that time period. In this case, it is absolutely fine only to go into detail about your most recent jobs, the jobs that you did for the longest time or the ones that are most relevant to what you are applying for now. Anything else can be summarised, as in the following example:

> Other jobs have included fruit picking, factory work and cooking in a fast food outlet. A full record can be provided on request.

This shows that you are not hiding anything, but you don't want to waste the selector's time with a long list of irrelevant material.

Will graduate employers really be interested in jobs that are completely unrelated to the one I am applying for now?

They may not be interested in the jobs as such – but they will be interested in the transferable skills that you have gained from them. This is why skills-based CVs often work best for mature students: they emphasise skills and personal qualities rather than dates and job titles.

If you prefer to use a chronological CV, you can still note these skills briefly, even for non-relevant jobs:

> Other jobs have included fruit picking, factory work and cooking in a fast food outlet, all of which show my ability to fit in quickly to different teams and to work under pressure. A full record can be provided on request.

Should I give details of my family, marital status or children?

Not specifically – in the past, people often did include personal details such as 'Marital status: Married, three children aged 11, 9 and 6' on their CVs but this would certainly not be expected today! However, this doesn't mean that you need to suppress any mention of your family or personal life in your application: just make sure that you only do this where it is relevant. This may account for what would otherwise be gaps in your career history, or may be volunteering or other responsibilities related to your children and their education, health or activities.

2006–2012
Full-time parent and part-time playgroup volunteer

The following CV shows how a mature student might use a skills-based CV to apply for a new field of work.

Nikki Clark

142 Northlands Road, Ellesmere Port,
Cheshire CH65 9KN
nclark771@mail.com   07700 900022

EDUCATION AND QUALIFICATIONS

1

University of Chester, LLB Law   **2014–2017**

Qualifying Law Degree with optional modules on Human Rights, Family Law and Commercial Law. Second year grade: 2.1

Warrington Collegiate   **2013–2014**
Access to Higher Education – Humanities & Social Sciences

Covered Law, Criminology, English and Psychology. Final Grade: Distinction.

RELEVANT EXPERIENCE

2

Cheshire Disability Advice Service   **2012 to date**
- Volunteer adviser, assisting clients with benefits advice, renewals and appeals.

Interengtech Ltd, Chester   **January – March 2016**
- As part of the Law Experiential Project LLB module I undertook a practical placement in a company legal department where I assisted with contract and employment law issues.

Marshalling   **June 2016**
- Shadowed a judge, observing a commercial dispute in the County Court and discussing the case with her.

SKILLS

3

Communication and customer service
- Used empathy and listening skills to advise clients of the Disability Advice Service.
- As a hairdresser, built up good working relationships with clients, offering advice on hair issues and being a good listener.

TEAMWORKING
- Worked with a group of five other students to prepare arguments for a mock trial.
- Cooperated with other parents, teachers and governors on the PTA of my children's school.

4

Negotiation

- As assistant manager of a hair salon, I arranged staff rotas and resolved problems with dissatisfied clients.
- Negotiated on behalf of clients with disabilities in relation to benefit claims.

Analytical skills

- As part of my LLB Law experiential project, I completed an assignment which critically evaluated the relationship between legal theory and my practical experience of employment law.

Commercial awareness

- As a self-employed business person, I have handled my own accounts and tax returns and complied with all relevant legislation.
- Developed my business through leafleting and promotions.

Time management

- Combined work as a freelance hairdresser with study, volunteering and family responsibilities.
- Worked in a busy hair salon where I successfully combined styling work with management responsibilities.

EMPLOYMENT HISTORY

Self-employed Mobile Hairdresser   **2000 to date**

- Providing hairdressing services in clients' homes

Hale Scissors, Hale, Greater Manchester   **1994–2000**

- Joined as apprentice and was promoted to junior stylist, stylist and senior stylist.
- As senior stylist, took on additional responsibilities as Assistant Salon Manager.

Interests

- Committee member of Ashgrove School Parent-Teacher Association.
- Canoeing and paddleboarding.

5

Notes on Nikki Clark's CV

1. As a law student, Nikki Clark is targeting her CV on law firms and other employers in the legal profession. These employers are often quite traditional and will be interested in her degree studies and relevant experience, so she begins her CV with these sections before moving on to her skills.
2. Although Nikki's relevant experience has so far all been voluntary, she gives it a prominent position in her CV and treats it as seriously as if it had been paid work. This shows employers that she considers this experience important and encourages them to value it as well.
3. Nikki then moves on to her skills, demonstrating a mixture of people and business skills through her varied experiences. Clients and client care are just as important to law firms as they are to hairdressing salons!
4. This brief mention of Nikki's children is in the context of her involvement with the school PTA. There is no real need to mention the children here – she could just have written 'Cooperated with parents, teachers and governors on the PTA of a local school' – but she may wish to let employers know that she does have children, without making it a major statement in her CV.
5. Nikki's work as a self-employed hairdresser may actually have been very occasional or part-time while her children were small but, by not going into unnecessary detail about this, she keeps the chronological part of her CV continuous without being misleading in any way.

Poor academic results

Graduates with a low degree class or disappointing A-level grades often blame these when their job applications are unsuccessful. If you are in this position, you may feel that you have only two options: either to lie about your results and 'improve' your grades or to leave them off your CV altogether.

We strongly advise against either of these options! As discussed in Chapter 2, lying on your CV could lead to any job offer being withdrawn and, if you have already started work before being found out, you could legally be dismissed.

Leaving your grades off your CV is not a good idea either. Employers know that people with good grades will make the most of them, so they will assume that anyone who doesn't include them doesn't have good grades! They may even assume that your grades are worse than they are.

A better strategy is to (1) target employers who don't put such a high priority on academic grades and (2) sell yourself on the basis of your skills and experience rather than your academic results. Not all employers require 2.1 degrees and 320 UCAS points: it is usually the most high-profile and popular graduate recruiters who use academic grades as a way to keep numbers of candidates down to a manageable level. Small and medium-sized employers (SMEs) are much more flexible and more willing to look at all parts of a graduate's application. They often prefer someone who they see as down-to-earth, good with all kinds of people, willing to 'muck in' and ready to learn, rather than someone whose main selling point is their academic track record.

This is the case even in popular and competitive areas such as the media. SMEs include many media employers such as publishers, public relations agencies and television production companies. Someone who has good practical skills and a realistic insight into the media, through editing the student newspaper or running the university radio station, will be of much greater interest than someone who has a 2.1 but a much lower level of experience.

Don't get fixated on your grades or put all your rejections down to them. Go back to Chapters 2 and 3, and think about everything else that you have to offer – your skills and experiences – anything you might need to do to develop or enhance these and how you can put them over to employers.

Several years ago I interviewed a Theology graduate who had just been awarded a 3rd class degree. He was a bit despondent about this but had a really pleasant outgoing personality and a conscientious attitude to everything he did.

A few months later I bumped into him again. He was really happy. He had taken a stop-gap job in a department store where he had impressed his manager with his hard work, cheerful demeanour, his desire to go out of his way to help customers, keenness to learn and positive attitude to even the most routine tasks. She had recommended him for the company management training scheme and he had just started on this programme.

—University careers adviser

All the 'problems' outlined in this chapter are quite common and none of them are insurmountable. You are not alone, and many graduates have overcome similar problems in the past, so there is help and advice out there. Talk to your careers adviser and use online support groups such as those listed at https://www.kent.ac.uk/ces/student/Disability%20-%20Useful%20 Links.pdf

Finding out more

1. TARGETJobs (2016) *How to market your gap year to graduate employers,* https://targetjobs.co.uk/internships/275493-how-to-market-your-gap-year-to-graduate-employers

2. TARGETJobs (2014) *Disability and mental health,* https://targetjobs.co.uk/ careers-advice/equality-and-diversity/320153-disability-and-mental-health-diversity-matters

3. Disability Rights UK (2015) *Careers and work for disabled people,* http:// www.disabilityrightsuk.org/careers-and-work-disabled-people#nine.

Chapter 14

Job hunting tips and how to submit your CV

Contents

What will you learn from this chapter?

So now you have written your CV and covering letter, what next? Do you email it or send it by post? What format do you send it in? How will employers and recruitment agencies deal with your CV? And what if you get rejected? There are many applicants for most jobs, so you have to learn how to cope with rejection.

Emailing your CV

The standard method for sending your CV is by email. In the subject line of the email, say which vacancy you are applying for, as large organisations may have many open vacancies. Put your covering letter in the body of your email, and keep the formatting simple so that it can be read by any email system.

Emails are not as easy to read as letters, so stick to short paragraphs with plenty of spacing. Give each point you make a new paragraph, with a gap between paragraphs.

Your CV is sent as an attachment, and you can also attach a nicely formatted version of your letter in MS Word or PDF format if you wish to (but see Chapter 12 on covering letters for the pros and cons of this). Give your CV a descriptive file name: 'Alan Davies CV' or 'Marketing vacancy ref 2091.doc' rather than 'CV.doc', so it can easily be found on filing systems.

Common mistakes made when emailing CVs

- Accidentally clicking 'Send' before the email is ready
- Making embarrassing spelling and grammatical mistakes
- Forgetting to attach the CV
- Forgetting to use 'blind copy' (BCC)

One candidate accidentally included a kiss icon at the end of her letter.

Keep a list of all the vacancies you have applied to and responses you have received so you can follow up if necessary.

Vacancy	Employer	Reference	Date Sent	Response Received	Comments
Trainee PR Executive	Viaduct	V2035	18.10.16	28.10.16	Invited for telephone interview

In which format should you submit your CV?

Some recruiters specify that the CV must be in a particular format: if you ignore this, you risk rejection on the grounds that you can't follow instructions, but for most employers, the only important factor is their ability to read the CV easily.

PDF (portable document format)

PDF is commonly used for CVs because it preserves formatting and PDF readers are widely available. MS Word has a PDF export function. PDF is also better for designer CVs, as fonts, graphics and formatting aren't altered.

PDF files look as you intended them to, no matter what computer is used to view the CV; they are also secure and can't easily be altered by the recruiter, although this can be a problem if a recruitment consultant needs to edit your CV by, for example, removing contact details before forwarding it to the hiring manager.

MS Word (.docx) format

MS Word is the most commonly used format for sending CVs. Some employers prefer Word format as they can easily add notes to the file to refer to at interview. Word documents can also be opened in Open Office and LibreOffice.

There are also disadvantages. Word files may contain sensitive information such as previous versions of the CV, and Word documents can contain macro viruses. Your CV may render differently in different versions of Word and on different computer systems, changing appearance and formatting, so check its appearance on several computers before sending it out. Another problem is that if you make what MS Word thinks is a spelling or grammatical error, it will underline this in colour, even if this is intentional, such as writing 'Managed . . .' instead of 'I managed . . .'

Advantages and disadvantages of MS Word and PDF format CVs	
PDF	**MS Word**
+ Looks the same on all computers	+ Can be opened by many word processors
+ Most word processors can convert files to PDF	+ Employers can easily add notes
– Can't be easily edited (this can also be a plus point)	– Appearance may vary on different computers
	– May show underlining of 'mistakes'

Other formats

Rich Text Format (.rtf) can be opened by nearly all word-processing packages, but few recruiters like it. Don't submit your CV in other formats **such as Open Document Text** (.odt), **Apple Mac .pages** or **Latex**, as some computers can't open these. Instead convert your CV to PDF or Word format before sending.

Web CVs use HTML format and allow you to include the web address of your CV in emails. They allow graphics, colour, hyperlinks and even sound, animation and video. Web CVs show that you are up to date with technology and are effective for web design jobs by demonstrating your technical prowess.

Text-only CVs

Once you have submitted your CV, you have no control over how it is processed. It might be scanned and the contents fed into a database leading to mangled content. Plain text which has all the formatting stripped out is the least likely to suffer from this.

A plain text version of your CV also allows you to copy text quickly into the boxes on an online application form, and occasionally companies may want the entire CV as a text file. A few employers are reluctant to accept CVs as attachments because of worries about viruses, and may specify a text CV submitted in the body of your email. These don't look attractive but can be read on any computer. Where a plain text is required:

- You can't use bold, italic, underlining or different fonts and sizes, so use CAPITAL LETTERS for headings.
- You can't use proper bullets, so use asterisks* instead.
- Careful spacing can enhance the clarity and looks.
- You can use a series of dashes to separate sections
  -

Example beginning of a text CV

```
JOHN ANDREWS

6 Earl Road, London, SW1 8NP    Email: jma555@kent.ac.uk

EDUCATION
BSc (Hons) Computer Science, University of Kent,
2013-2016

Modules include:
* Software Engineering
* Computer Networks and Communications
```

So which format should you use?

One survey of recruiters found that:

- 63 per cent preferred **MS Word** .docx format.
- 36 per cent preferred **Adobe Acrobat** .pdf format.

- Only one per cent preferred **rich-text** .rtf format, and none preferred **text** format (.txt) or **web** page format (.html).

MS Word and PDF are by far the most common formats. One strategy is to attach your CV in both Word and PDF formats and to allow employers to choose which they prefer.

Paper CVs

CVs are now rarely sent by post, and many offices no longer have space to file paper documents, but, if you've tried everything else, you could try posting a speculative application, as its novelty value may give it a better chance of being read.

Paper CVs are also useful for handing out to recruiters at careers fairs and to retailers or restaurants for casual work. It's also wise to bring a paper copy of your CV to interview in case the interviewer has not got a good copy. If your CV is more than one page in length, print it on one side of the paper only, so the recruiter doesn't have to keep turning it over to read it: the recruiter can place both sheets side by side to view the whole CV, but put your name in the footer of each page in case the pages get separated.

One chemistry graduate sent handwritten letters of application through the post instead of emailing his CV. He had beautiful calligraphic handwriting, and his warm writing style helped his personality to shine through. Most professionals get many emails every day but rarely receive letters, so a carefully written and researched letter may just attract more attention.

Recruitment agencies

Recruitment agencies are used by large employers to spread their net widely and by smaller ones which don't have the resources to carry out their own recruitment. Employers using agencies often want candidates with substantial work experience, which can limit opportunities for new graduates.

Research agencies to find the right ones for you: some specialise in particular job sectors, and some do specialise in graduates. It's worth sending your CV to several agencies as some may not respond. Others may offer you a telephone 'screening interview', where a consultant questions you to see if you would be suitable to send to interviews with clients.

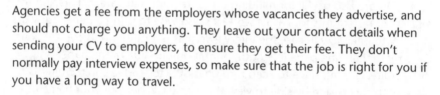

Trainee copywriter required for leading advertising agency, salary £40,000

A few agencies advertise non-existent dream jobs to produce a pool of candidates. This technique is also used by job scammers, so if an advert seems too good to be true, check it very carefully.

Agencies get a fee from the employers whose vacancies they advertise, and should not charge you anything. They leave out your contact details when sending your CV to employers, to ensure they get their fee. They don't normally pay interview expenses, so make sure that the job is right for you if you have a long way to travel.

Social media

It's wise to have your CV on LinkedIn as this is by far the most popular social media site for recruitment. LinkedIn profiles with a photo are much more likely to be viewed, but make sure your photo looks professional – a head and shoulders shot in smart clothing – and smile! If you wish to join someone's LinkedIn network, compose a personalised message saying why you wish to link, rather than just sending the standard 'I'd like to join your LinkedIn network', which can turn people off.

The following are not needed by employers and can lead to identity theft, so leave them out.

- Place and date of birth
- Address
- Marital status
- Your middle name (you only need to give your first and last names)

Check your digital footprint

Make sure that your **Facebook** page doesn't carry evidence of any indiscretions that employers might view, and keep your page private and viewable only by friends. Increasingly, companies check candidates' digital footprints, starting with their LinkedIn profile, and they may also Google you to check for inconsistencies between your CV and online content.

CV templates

Many websites offer CV templates: skeleton CVs where you add your own content. These can look good and work as a quick fix if you need a CV in a hurry, but they stifle your initiative and creativity with a one-size-fits-all approach, and they aren't tailored to your circumstances. It can also be difficult to change their structure and order, so they end up being longer than required. In addition, templates make you appear bland and ordinary rather than unique and extraordinary.

Coping with rejection

Job hunting can be a long and stressful process, and it rarely takes a direct route from your first application to a job offer. Rejection is a normal part of the job-hunting process, so you must learn not to take this personally. Typically, about one in ten candidates gets an interview for a job.

Regularly review your progress. How successful have you been in getting interviews?

If you haven't heard back about a job you have applied to, it's fine to email the employer to ask why: it may be that your application is still in the system, and recruiters might be encouraged by your interest. If you have been rejected, you can ask for feedback on why you were unsuccessful. You are unlikely to get detailed feedback but might get some useful pointers.

Dear Ms Byrne,

Thank you for letting me know that I wasn't successful in my application. Although I am obviously disappointed, I do appreciate that you had a number of good applicants to choose from.

Would you be able to give me some more specific detail on why I was rejected and how I may be able to improve? This would help me greatly with future applications.

I would be most grateful if you could keep me in mind for any future vacancies which may arise, as I would love the opportunity to work for your company.

Yours sincerely,
Ravindra Desai

If you are persistent, you will almost always eventually succeed, but if you are unsuccessful over a long period, try applying for alternatives which are easier to enter. Competition for marketing jobs can be intense, but sales roles, which can be a stepping stone into marketing, may be much easier to get.

In the course of job hunting, you may stumble across appealing roles that you never even knew existed, so it pays to pursue interesting alternatives when they come up.

While you are looking for work after University, divide each day into periods to give your days a structure: job hunting is a full-time job!

Monday							
9 a.m.	10 a.m.	11 a.m.	12 noon	1 p.m.	2 p.m.	3 p.m.	4 p.m.
Research law jobs on the Web		Write letter for job X		Lunch	Improve LinkedIn profile		Networking

The following chart will give you lots of strategies to help you to cope if your job hunting is initially unsuccessful.

FIGURE 14.1 Coping with rejection.

Most importantly, get help from your university careers service, who will be able to give you advice, review your strategy, critique your CV and application forms and help with career choice and sources of jobs to apply to.

Finding out more

Book

Kelly, M. (2015) *Social Media for Your Student and Graduate Job Search* (Basingstoke and New York: Palgrave Macmillan).

List of graduate recruitment agencies

www.kent.ac.uk/careers/recruit.htm

So what next?

Contents

What will you learn from this chapter?

Your CV is just the first stage in the process of getting a job. It's also important to keep developing your CV, even after you have found your first job: the job market is changing constantly and research carried out in Australia[1] predicts that people born between 1995 and 2009 will have 17 jobs across five different careers during their lifetime. The lessons you've learned in this book should help you throughout your working life.

Your CV is just one step in the process

> Great things are done by a series of small things brought together.
> —*Vincent Van Gogh*

However good your CV is, you are unlikely to be offered a job on the strength of this alone. A CV is just the first stage in getting a job and would normally be followed by an interview – possibly more than one. In larger organisations, you might also have to complete aptitude tests and an assessment centre.

Although this book is about CVs, much of what you have learned will be relevant to later stages in the job-hunting process. Knowing how to research jobs and employers will help you to answer application form and interview questions such as 'Why do you want to work for us?' and 'What attracts you to this role?' The work you have done analysing your skills and achievements will have prepared you for the competency interviews typically faced by graduates.

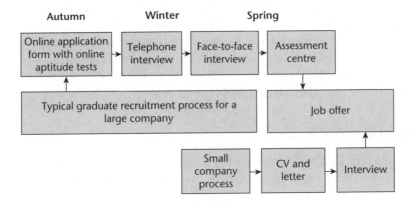

Before an interview

Reread your CV as if you were the interviewer. Think about these issues:

- How might the recruiter use your CV to decide on questions to ask you?
- What parts of your CV are most important in relation to this job?
- What are your weak points? What parts of your CV would you rather *not* be asked about? Employers are likely to hone in on these, so prepare your answers in advance. This will help you to tackle difficult questions more confidently.
- Update your research on the employer – have there been any new developments since you sent in your CV?

Keep developing your CV

The skills you have learned here to produce an extremely high-quality CV will not become redundant once you have gained your first job! They will continue to be useful throughout your working life – and not just to apply for future jobs as your career progresses. The skills required to produce a strong CV and covering letter, such as writing succinctly and putting across a persuasive argument concisely and clearly, will also help you when writing reports and business communications.

Once you have successfully made your first career move, don't forget about your CV! It is a good idea to review it every six months or so, adding in new skills learned and experience gained and deciding which parts of your experience from further back in your life can now be dropped from your CV.

Maintaining your CV in this way will help you to measure how your career is progressing and to pinpoint attributes you need to develop to move forward in your career. You may be able to use this at workplace appraisals. It also means that your CV is always up to date for when you are ready to make your next career move: you may need to make an application at short notice. Don't forget to update your LinkedIn profile as well.

Final CV Quiz

This is a final quiz to see how much you have learned from the book. Answer True or False to each question (answers are at the end of the chapter).

	True	False
1. A CV can be used for any job application.		
2. The more CVs you send out, the better your chances.		
3. 'Education' and 'Qualifications' should be separate sections on a CV.		
4. Action words such as 'organised', 'initiated', 'persuaded' and 'coordinated' make a good impression on employers.		
5. When applying abroad, you should prepare your CV in the language of the country in question.		
6. Your CV should be laid out in reverse chronological order (most recent items first).		
7. A CV should never be more than one page long.		
8. A brightly coloured CV will attract attention and improve your chances.		
9. You do not have to put all the jobs you have had on your CV.		
10. You should compose a different CV for each different type of employer.		

CV Checklist

Once you have prepared your CV, use the following checklist to check it. If you score 30 or more, you are probably well on the way to a brilliant CV!

Layout

❑ Is your CV no more than two pages long?
❑ Hold it at arm's length: does it look smart and professional?
❑ Is everything neatly aligned?
❑ Is it easy and clear to read – not cramped?
❑ Is there at least a line of white space between sections?
❑ Are there any paragraphs of seven lines or longer? Paragraphs that are too long may not be read, so break them up into shorter sections.
❑ Is it in reverse chronological order (most recent things first)?
❑ Are the page margins at least 1.25 cm all round?

Style

❑ Are you using proper bullets for lists?
❑ Have you included course modules, projects and relevant skills?
❑ Are no more than two different fonts used?
❑ Are you using larger font sizes for subheadings such as Education?
❑ Are **bold** or *italic* used rather than <u>underlining</u> to emphasise key points?

Spelling and Grammar

❑ Have you used a spellchecker (set to UK English if applying for jobs in the United Kingdom)?
❑ Have you also proofread your CV thoroughly – and asked somebody else to proofread it for you?
❑ Are you using capitalisation and punctuation correctly?
❑ Is the writing lively, with action words?

Structure

❑ Are there clearly identified sections, such as 'Work Experience'?
❑ Do the most important sections come first? Most student and graduate CVs will start with 'Education', but if you have relevant and significant work experience, it might be better to put this section first.

❑ Is all the information about a particular topic together in one place? For example, the places where you studied and the qualifications that you achieved there should be under a single 'Education' heading.

Personal details

❑ Have you put your name at the top in a large font size so the selector can easily pick out your CV?

❑ Is your email address sensible and businesslike?

Work experience

❑ Have you described key tasks, responsibilities and skills gained from work experience?

Skills

❑ Have you mentioned foreign languages, computing and driving?

❑ Have you given examples of skills relevant to the job you are applying for?

Interests

❑ Have you included a range of interests?

❑ Have you included social and active interests rather than just solitary and passive interests?

❑ Is there evidence of serious commitment to at least one activity?

❑ Is there organising or leadership experience, evidence of taking responsibility or initiative?

❑ Have you mentioned any interests relevant to the job?

Referees

❑ Have you thought about whether you should include full details of your referees? You don't normally need to do this unless specifically asked.

Feedback

❑ Have you asked someone with knowledge of recruitment practices, or of that job sector, for feedback? Careers advisers, friends or relatives, academic staff or previous employers may all be able to help here.

Quiz answers

1. *A CV can be used for any job application.*
   False. Don't use a CV if the employer has specified that candidates should complete their own application form.

2. *The more CVs you send out, the better your chances.*
   False – unless all your CVs are carefully researched and targeted.

3. *'Education' and 'Qualifications' should be separate sections on a CV.*
   False. It is much easier for the reader if these are put together in one section rather than making them hop back and forth between different sections to find out what you studied where.

4. *Action words such as 'organised', 'initiated', 'persuaded' and 'coordinated' make a good impression on employers.*
   True – if backed up by evidence in the form of concrete examples of where you have displayed these.

5. *When applying abroad you should prepare your CV in the language of the country in question.*
   True. There may even be a prevailing style of CV which is preferred – for example French CVs normally include a photograph, whereas this is unusual in the United Kingdom. If applying to a British company abroad, however, a British CV may do.

6. *Your CV should be laid out in reverse chronological order.*
   True – unless you are using a skills-based CV.

7. *A CV should never be more than one page long.*
   False. One side is fine if you can manage it, but it is better to have two sides of well-laid-out, easy-to-read information than one side of cramped and crowded print.

8. *A brightly coloured CV will attract attention and improve your chances.*
   False. Well, it may attract attention, but not the sort of attention that will improve your chances!

9. *You don't have to put all the jobs you have had on your CV.*
   True. It is the relevance of the jobs you have had or the skills you can demonstrate from them that are important.

10. *You should compose a different CV for each different type of employer.*
    True, ideally, although this may not always be possible if you have
    very limited information on the employer. The main point is that
    CVs for different careers would be different depending on the skills
    required.

Well done if you got all ten right!

Some final words from recruiters and jobseekers

*At one interview, the employer told me how impressed she was with my CV. She liked the
fact that it was clearly laid out and made it easy for her to pick out my skills and experience
at a glance.*

*As a recruiter, to get a CV that is completely free of spelling and grammatical errors is a
breath of fresh air in a day when I see hundreds of these errors and will always prejudice
me in that candidate's favour.*

*At first, you think sending a CV is the easy way to get a job and that it's much less time and
trouble than filling out all those online forms for different employers. But you do still need to
take time and trouble for your CV to stand out from all the others.*

*Application forms always have a big section headed 'Work Experience' or 'Employment
History' and I didn't have any proper experience to put in this section. Using a CV meant
that I could use other things I had done, like sports and travelling, to show what I could do.*

*It doesn't matter how brilliant your degree or what you've achieved – your CV needs to
show how all that will help you to do the job.*

As we mentioned at the start of this book, the graduate job market is
competitive and CVs need to be done well. We hope that this book
has improved your knowledge of what makes a good CV, has inspired
you to create your own in a style that makes the most of your skills and
experience, and will help you too to achieve success in your chosen
career.

Good luck!

Finding out more

Other useful books in the Palgrave Career Skills series

Woodcock, B. (2016) *Excel at Graduate Interviews.*

Houston, K. and E. Cunningham (2015) *How to Succeed at Assessment Centres.*

Rook, S. (2015) *Work Experience, Placements and Internships.*

References

1. McCrindle Research (2015) The Future of Work: Technology, Innovation and Collaboration, 23 September, http://bit.ly/2aTlQ49.

Index